Zero to 1 in 4 Seconds [3 in 1]

The Collection of Ready-to-Use Information for Young Entrepreneurs Who Want to Get the Million-Dollar Idea

By

Nespy Online Marketing

© **Copyright 2021 by Nespy Online Marketing-All rights reserved.**

This document is geared towards providing exact and reliable information regarding the topic and issue covered. The publication is sold with the idea that the publisher is not required to render accounting, officially permitted, or otherwise qualified services. If advice is necessary, legal or professional, a practiced individual in the profession should be ordered. From a Declaration of Principles which was accepted and approved equally by a Committee of the American Bar Association and a Committee of Publishers and Associations. In no way is it legal to reproduce, duplicate, or transmit any part of this document in either electronic means or in printed format. Recording of this publication is strictly prohibited and any storage of this document is not allowed unless with written permission from the publisher. All rights reserved. The information provided herein is stated to be truthful and consistent, in that any liability, in terms of inattention or otherwise, by any usage or abuse of any policies, processes, or Instructions contained within is the solitary and utter responsibility of the recipient reader. Under no circumstances will any legal responsibility or blame be held against the publisher for any reparation, damages, or monetary loss due to the information herein, either directly or indirectly. Respective authors own all copyrights not held by the publisher. The information herein is offered for informational purposes solely and is universal as so. The presentation of the information is without contract or any type of guarantee assurance. The trademarks that are used are without any consent and the publication of the trademark is without permission or backing by the trademark owner. All trademarks and brands within this book are for clarifying purposes only and are the owned by the owners themselves, not affiliated with this document.

Author: Nespy Online Marketing

The Golden Inner Circle is an elitist group business incubator. It's a way to speed yourself up with far fewer setbacks. If you are already on track follow these enlighten entrepreneurs to take you to the next level of your potential.

Get the support you need to:

- free yourself from negative limiting beliefs

- develop a marketing strategy that works

- discover the Golden Method to improve your skills

- realize the dream of being able to work in complete autonomy

- create passive income with low-budget investments form your home.

The Golden Inner Circle is the movement that is leading hundreds of people to find a real strategy to achieve great results in the most profitable businesses such as Youtube, Instagram, Airbnb…

This series of over 20 books called "Clever Entrepreneurs in the XXI Century" is a step-by-step program that will take you from zero to the highest level of success.

The information contained within will help you to raise the dormant leader inside you, develop the King Midas' touch and to embody the NEW Golden YOU.

Table of Contents

The Complete Startup Crash Course

Introduction	13
CHAPTER 1: Lean Start-up	16
1.1 Learn to build a Lean Start-up	18
CHAPTER 2: Importance of Market Research	25
2.1 Develop an understanding of the Market Research	26
2.2 Collection of information through Market Research	26
CHAPTER 3: Digital Entrepreneurship	32
CHAPTER 4: The Best Business	40
4.1 Start your own online Dropshipper business	41
4.2 How to Find and Work with Reliable Dropshipping Suppliers	51
Conclusion	75

The 9+1 Best Home-Based Business Model of 2021

Introduction	81
CHAPTER 1: The Nirma Washing Powder's Success Story	84
1.1 Invention of Nirma detergent?	85
1.2 Karsanbhai Patel's sale policy for Nirma detergent	87
1.3 Invest In Research and Development	88
1.4 No Higher Costs	89

1.5 Be Proactive in your approach as it is beneficial for the business — 90

1.6 Provide Customers with 'Value for Money' — 91

1.7 Define Your Segment — 91

1.8 Focus on Building a Brand — 92

1.9 Astutely Manage the Brand Wars — 93

1.10 Diversify the Portfolio — 95

1.11 Conclusion — 96

1.12 What Karsanbhai Patel and Nirma detergent did for the Indian Economy — 97

1.13 Karsanbhai Patel's ventures other than the Nirma detergent — 97

CHAPTER 2: Start a Profitable Soap Making Business — 99

2.1 What will you name your business? — 104

2.2 Form a legal entity — 104

2.3 Small Business Taxes — 105

2.4 Open a business bank account & credit card — 105

2.5 Open a business bank account — 105

2.6 Get a business credit card — 106

2.7 Obtain necessary permits and licenses — 106

2.8 State & Local Business Licensing Requirements	106
2.9 Labor safety requirements	107
2.10 Certificate of Occupancy	107
2.11 Trademark & Copyright Protection	108
2.12 Get business insurance	108
2.13 Learn more about General Liability Insurance	108
2.14 Define your brand	109
2.15 Soap Making Plan	110
2.16 Soap selling process	118
2.17 Soap making supplies	119
2.18 Marketing area for soap	120
2.19 Total investment	120
2.20 Selling price	121
2.21 Profit margin	121
2.22 Precaution	122
2.23 Risk	122
2.24 Conclusion	122
2.25 Advantage of starting a soap making business at home	122
2.26 How Much Money Can You Make Making Soap?	123

CHAPTER 3: Start a Profitable Candle Making Business   125

    3.1 Steps for starting a candle making business   125

    3.2 How much can you charge customers?   129

    3.3 Benefits of candle making business   139

Conclusion   141

Private Label Crash Course

Introduction   146

Chapter 1: Getting Started-Private Label   151

    1.1 What is Private Label?   152

    1.2 Private Label Categories   152

    1.3 Different types of Private Label as profitable strategies   153

    1.4 White Label vs. Private Label Dropshipping?   154

    1.5 Dropshipping Private Label   157

    1.6 Deciding What to Private Label   159

Chapter 2: Profitable Strategies in Building Six-Figure Business   166

    2.1 Private Label for Profitability   166

    2.2 9+1 Pricing Strategies   170

    2.3 Best Practices in Private Label Branding   175

2.4 Positives and Negatives of Private Label   178

2.5 Keys to Private Label Greatness   180

Chapter 3: Finding the Products & Starting Your Personal Brand   185

3.1 How to Start Your Private Label Brand from Scratch?   186

3.2 Understand the costs of private labeling   188

3.3 Choosing the Right Products   198

3.4 Building a Team and Starting your Personal Brand   201

Conclusion   207

The Complete Startup Crash Course

How Digital Entrepreneurs Use Continuous Innovation to Create Radically Successful Businesses and How You Can Copy Them

By

Nespy Online Marketing

Table of Contents

Introduction — 13

CHAPTER 1: Lean Start-up — 16

   1.1 Learn to build a Lean Start-up — 18

CHAPTER 2: Importance of Market Research — 25

   2.1 Develop an understanding of the Market Research — 26

   2.2 Collection of information through Market Research — 26

CHAPTER 3: Digital Entrepreneurship — 32

CHAPTER 4: The Best Business — 40

   4.1 Start your own online Dropshipper business — 41

   4.2 How to Find and Work with Reliable Dropshipping Suppliers — 51

Conclusion — 75

Introduction

An entrepreneur is a clever fellow who wants to create an enterprise in circumstances of intense complexity. More than often, a company's priorities don't always fit the ways people need or want a service or product. New products and new projects stall at some stage or don't live up to their full potential. It is where the Lean Startup model comes in. The core philosophy behind the Lean Startup model, which is an evolution of astute businessmen's management style, promotes an atmosphere that allows new concepts to thrive while finding ways to reduce waste. Sometimes as challenging as it may be, the only way ahead might be to ditch what you have and start again from scratch. In stagnation or unfavorable economic conditions, we all are advised to do something for less. All of you must be well aware of the idea of having to do a great many things with little money along with reinventing ourselves or our systems to cater to the ever-changing needs of our consumers. Astute entrepreneurs have insight plus know means and strategies of evaluating success.

Additionally, they can determine the next steps of action, find shortcomings, and make commensurate changes to change with the changing circumstances and atmosphere to develop and further innovate. It is generally accepted that hard work and determination, combined with historical predictors, are automatic performance measures. However, the future is uncertain, and the old methods of working are just not applicable. The management of the previous century does not work with the instability of today's economy. Frustrated with conventional strategies and approaches to entrepreneurship, the creative entrepreneurs begin looking for other ideas to bring to the test. They all have come up with the Lean Startup model that focuses on innovation and getting to know customers' needs and habits to create a better product or service. It focuses on the correct process, that is, to work better and not simply harder to solve difficult circumstances. Whether it is a start-up of tech, small businesses, or a project inside a big corporation, Launching a new organization has long been a hit-or-the-miss proposition. According to the decades-old formula, you always write a marketing strategy, pitch this to the investors, build a team, launch a product, & start to sell it as much as you possibly can. & somewhere in the chain of events, you will inevitably suffer fatal failure. Most of the time, the odds aren't in your favor. A recent study by Harvard Business School reveals that 75 percent of all start-ups crash. But lately, the important countervailing factor has arisen, one which can make the task of beginning a business less dangerous. It's a technique called the "leaned start-up," & it encourages experimentation over the elaborate organizing, customer input over intuition, & iterative designs over conventional "big designs upfront" expansion. While methodology's only a few years old, and its constructs like "minimum viable product" & "pivoting"— have rapidly taken hold in the start-up community, & business schools have already started modifying the curricula to explain them. The lean start-up movement is changing traditional thinking around entrepreneurship. Newest ventures of every sort try to boost the chances of survival by pursuing the ideals of struggling quickly and learning quickly. Despite methods name, some of the greatest payoffs can be earned by the major corporations that embrace it in the long run. This book shall explore in deep as to how digital entrepreneurs utilize continuous creativity to build fundamentally profitable companies and how you can imitate them.

CHAPTER 1: Lean Start-up

lean start-up is a strategy used on behalf of an established business to create new companies or launch a new product. Method of lean start-up advocates the development of products that customers have already shown they want so that as quick as product's launched, a market will already exist. It is in contrast to creating a brand and then hoping the demand would emerge. Developers of Product can measure consumers' interest in a product & determine how the product may need to be clarified by employing lean start-up principles. The process is referred to as validated learning & can be used to prevent unnecessary usage of the resources in the creation & development of products. If innovation is likely to be failed by lean start-ups, it'll fail cheaply and quickly instead of gradually & expensively, thence the word "fail-fast." Lean start-up's example of customers dictating the type of goods that the respective markets deliver, instead of deciding what products they would be provided.

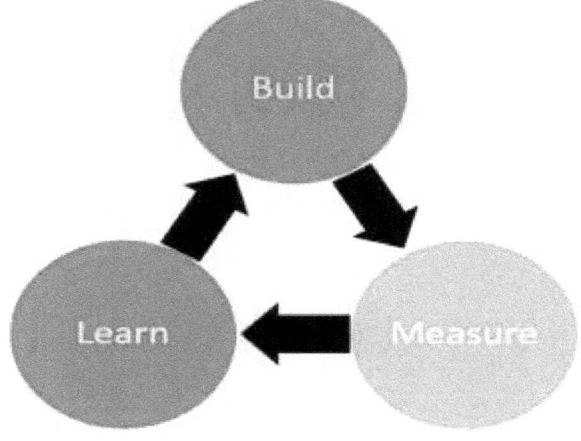

Lean Start-ups vs. the Traditional Businesses

When it comes to hiring, the lean entrepreneurship approach often differentiates itself from the conventional company model. Lean start-ups attract employees who can adapt, learn, and work efficiently, whereas conventional firms recruit employees based on knowledge and expertise. Lean start-ups employ multiple financial recording metrics also; they concentrate on the customer acquisition expenses, lifetime consumer value, client churn rate, & how viral the product maybe, instead of relying on revenue statements, balance sheets, and cash flow statements.

Requirements for the Lean Startup

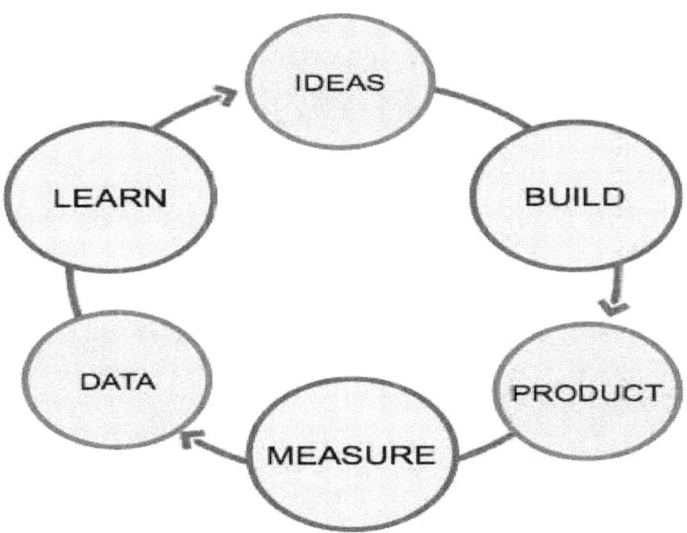

Experimentation is perceived by the lean start-up approach to be extra valuable than comprehensive planning. A waste of time is viewed as five years of business plans designed on unknowns, and consumer response is paramount. Instead of the business models, Lean start-ups use business concepts focused on assumptions that are easily checked. Before proceeding, data doesn't have to be completed; it only has to be more than enough. The start-up easily changes to limit the losses & return to the production of goods consumers want when customers do not respond. Failure is generally regarded as the rule. Following this strategy, entrepreneurs validate their theories by engaging with prospective consumers, investors, & partners to evaluate their responses to product specifications, packaging, delivery, and customer retention. With the data, entrepreneurs make tiny changes to goods called iterations, and big adjustments known as pivots fix any major issues. To best suit the current target consumer, this testing process could result in exchanging target customers or altering the product. A problem that must be addressed is first defined by the lean start-up method. It then produces the minimum workable product or smallest product type that enables entrepreneurs to offer prospective buyers. This strategy is simpler and less risky than checking final product production, and decreasing the risk that start-ups face reduces their usual high failure rate. Lean start-ups redefine start-up as an enterprise aiming for scalable growth models, not the one that is determined to follow an established business strategy.

1.1 Learn to build a Lean Start-up

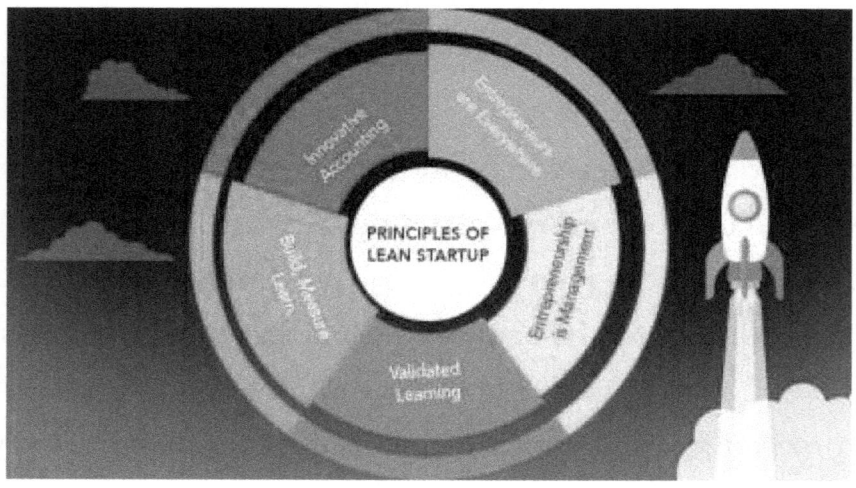

Do you know the 75 percent of all start-ups usually fail? You're likely to encounter obstacles, difficulties, and roadblocks of all sorts, no matter which type of company you're beginning to build. You could spend years on one business idea to fail if you've followed the conventional start-up formula of drafting a business plan, setting up to the investors, developing your product, & selling it. The Lean Startup Methodology is an inexpensive, fast, and less risky technique to carry your business concept to the market. Launching some form of business has always been risky. "Instead of using more traditional methods, the main distinction between building lean start-ups with Lean Start-ups Methodology is that entrepreneurs must ask themselves that "Should the products be built? "instead of "Can the products be built? It is about identifying a problem, validating the question, and creating a product that can fix the problem to create a lean start-up. When you create a lean start-up, you need to ensure that your product is consistently checked and verified, so your product's in the customer's hands as quick as possible. Subsequently, Lean Startups Methodology would help you optimize business growth. To begin creating a lean start-up, here are three moves entrepreneurs may take: Find, Execute, & Validate it.

Find the Business Idea

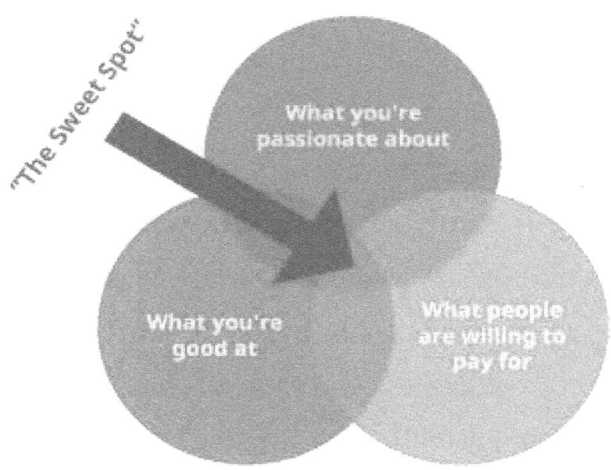

the big question is not: "could this be built?" or "Should this be built?" "It puts us in an extraordinary historical moment: the success of collective imaginations depends on our future prosperity. It's important to determine whether the product can fix is significant enough for clients to choose to buy it while selecting a company concept to pursue using the Lean Startup Approach. It can be easy to find a business idea, so it's essential to pay attention to the challenges people face daily. For the product to gain momentum, clients must be aggressively looking for solutions to a problem. It is time to execute the project after you settle on a business idea.

Execute the Business Idea

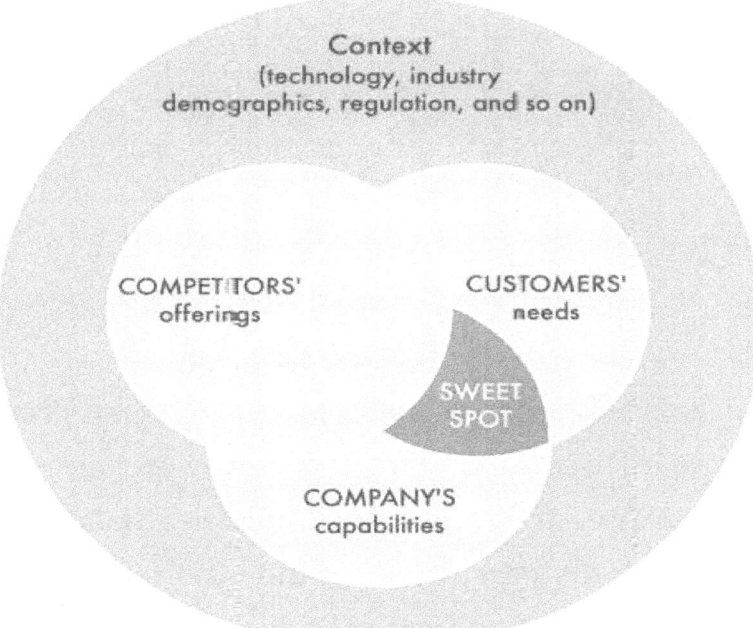

Next, you can create minimum viable products (MVP). MVP is a version of a product you plan to create, allowing the team to quickly gather as much knowledge as possible on your prospective consumers and their input on the product. Any Lean Start-up Philosophy advocates recommend that you take the "Kickstarter Approach" for your product, i.e., start selling the product before it's completed to build market value and drive demand in the product while collecting funds for the Lean Startup. It's time to validate the business plan once the business ideas are executed.

Validate the Business idea

4 STEPS FOR IDEA VALIDATION

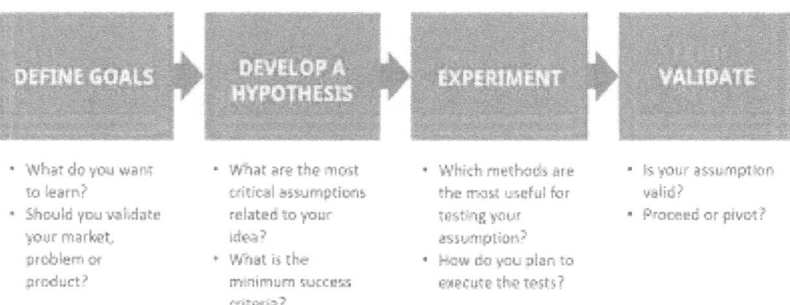

Start-ups do not only exist to make products, make profits, or even support clients. Their main target is to know how to create a profitable enterprise. By conducting multiple trials that allow the entrepreneurs to verify each aspect of the vision, this learning can be scientifically validated. Product validation's a crucial step in the development of profitable Lean Start-ups. In this phase, in the real world, it's time to play with the business idea. Early adopter or otherwise, test the MVP with actual consumers in the industry to see whether the product is feasible and to gain knowledge that you could study. Use this knowledge to determine if you can continue building your product, modifying the product, or pivoting your market plan. If the findings are mainly good from checking MVP in the marketplace, continue to develop your products using your initial approach while integrating tester input. If the outcomes of marketplace MVP research are favorable and unfavorable, tweak the product or business plan to make the product ideally suited to your consumers' desires and needs. If the findings are mainly disappointing from checking MVP in the industry, it's time for pivoting your product & business plan. To adapt vision to suit the desires and the needs of the clients would entail a radical change in your technique and work. Under certain circumstances, mainly unfavorable reviews would indicate that Lean Startup can fully quit the marketplace.

Why should one build a Lean Start-up?

Start-up's different way of seeing at the growth of innovative and new products, all at the same time highlighting rapid iteration & customer insights, huge vision & great ambition. Building a lean start-up is an ideal opportunity for entrepreneurs who need to start an inexpensive company and easily bring them to market. Building lean start-up essentially shortens product creation times and means that developers build products through experimentation & validated learning that satisfy consumer needs.

Example of Lean Startup

For instance, a healthy meal delivery service that targets busy, single twenty-somethings in the urban areas could learn that thirty-something wealthy mothers of newborns in the suburbs have a better market. The business could then alter its delivery schedule & the types of foods it serves to provide new mothers with optimal nutrition. It could also add options for spouses or partners & other children in the household for meals. The lean start-up approach is not intended to be used solely by start-ups. In developing countries where electricity is unreliable, companies such as General Electric have used the technique to develop a new battery for cell phone companies.

CHAPTER 2: Importance of Market Research

The method of evaluating a new product or service's feasibility through surveys carried out directly with prospective consumers is market research. Market analysis helps an organization discover the target market & collect customers' views and the other inputs on product or service participation. This form of research may be performed in-house through the organization itself or a 3rd party company specialising in market analysis. Through polls, product testing, & focus groups, it can be achieved. Usually, research subjects are compensated with the samples of goods or/and paid nominal stipends for the time. Market analysis is a vital aspect of new products or service's research and development (R&D).

The company uses market testing by engaging individuals with a prospective buyer to test its feasibility or service.

Companies will find out the target customers through market analysis and get customer reviews and input quickly.

This form of research may be performed in-house through the organization itself or an independent company specializing in the market analysis.

The study includes surveys, testing of products, & focus groups.

2.1 Develop an understanding of the Market Research

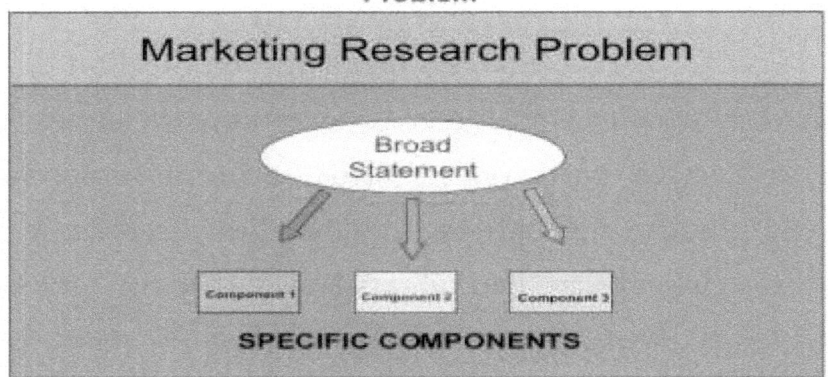

Figure 2.8 Proper Definition of the Marketing Research Problem

The market research aims to examine the market related to certain products or services to decide how the audience receives them. It will include the compilation of information for the market segmentation & product differentiation purposes that could be used to target promotional campaigns and assess what attributes are perceived as a concern by the customer. To complete the process of market analysis, an organization must participate in plenty of activities. Based on the business area being investigated, it needs to collect information. To assess the existence of certain trends or the related data point that it can use in decision-making, the organization needs to evaluate and understand the resulting data. Market research's a vital instrument for helping businesses identify what buyers expect, produce goods that people can use, & maintain a strategic edge over other businesses in their sector.

2.2 Collection of information through Market Research

The market analysis contains a mixture of the primary information, meaning what the organization or a person recruited by a company has collected, & secondary pieces of information, or what outside source has collected.

Primary Information

The Primary data is either compiled by the organization or gathered by an individual or a business contracted to do analysis. Generally speaking, this kind of knowledge falls into two categories: exploratory &/or specific research. Exploratory analysis is a less formal choice that works by many open-ended inquiries, resulting in the presentation of questions or challenges that might need to be answered by the enterprise. The relevant study seeks the solutions to questions previously understood that are mostly called to light by exploratory researches.

Secondary Information

Secondary data is data that has already been obtained from an external agency. It could include the demographic statistic from federal census results, research studies by trade groups, or research provided by the other organization working within the same business area.

Example of Market Research

Often firms use market analysis to evaluate potential ideas or gather customer knowledge on what types of products or the services they like and do not have at present. For instance, to test the feasibility of a product or service, a company considering going into the business might perform market research. If consumer interest is confirmed by market research, the company can proceed with the business plan confidently. If not, to make changes to the product to get it in line with consumer expectations, the organization should use market analysis findings.

Components of Market Research

The research of market involves the gathering of information about:

customers – for developing a customer profile

industry & market environment – for understanding factors that are external to the business

competitors – for developing competitor profiles.

Learn to research the industry and market environment

the business & market factors analysis will concentrate on knowledge regarding any legal, political, social, economic, and cultural problems or developments that may impact your organization. This external analysis will then be used to obtain knowledge about the composition of the target market, market differences, emerging market patterns, and where the new market prospects may lie. Research on the industry and business outlook could cover:

- Market size & trends
- Business regulations
- Marketing channels
- Market demographics (for example, age, gender, income)
- Sociographic (for example, beliefs & attitudes, lifestyle factors, interests).

Sources that can be used for collecting the data

- Pertinent business & industry associations
- Online trade journal
- Newspapers
- Council businesses support service
- Print media
- Television
- Industry expos along with trade shows

Regional councils & relevant state governmental departments (which is depending upon the industry)

consumer lists or Commercially sold marketing

search engines for Internet

Research the customers

To collect the relevant information about who your clients or future customers are, & what, where, when & how they shop, you can use consumer analysis.

Customer analysis will also provide you with useful insights into your consumers' perceptions towards your organization and your goods and services.

Research on customers may cover:

- Needs & expectations
- Social & lifestyle trends
- Attitude towards you
- Customer demographics (like age, income, gender)
- Attitudes towards your opponents.

Sources for researching customers

- Focus groups
- surveys & questionnaires for staff and customers
- Observations of the customer behavior
- Personal interviews
- Feedback on points-of-sale
- Sales staff
- Phone surveys
- Social media
- Development offices for local business (local council & independent)

Research the competitors

Your study into competitors will obtain data on current and future competitors. You will use your rival's data to gain knowledge such as the existing business advantages of your competitor, shortcomings in their sales tactics, & how their consumers view their goods and services. Analysis of competitors may cover:

- Present turnover & market shares
- Pricing structures and policies
- Products & services
- Branding, marketing, advertising

Sources for researching competitors

- Competitor marketing & advertising material, the price-lists
- Past clients
- Suppliers
- Official offices like licensing bodies
- Business directories
- Competitor stores, pages on social media, and websites
- Complaints blogs & chat sites
- Competitor print & lists of electronic mailing
- Personal & staff observations

CHAPTER 3: Digital Entrepreneurship

It is important to academic study to consider the conditions and reasons that promote digital entrepreneurship (DE) and to direct market practice and public policies aimed at promoting this development, given its positive impacts on job development and economic growth. Digital entrepreneurship is a concept that determines how entrepreneurship can evolve as digital technology begins to disrupt industry and culture. Digital entrepreneurship illustrates trends in the practice, philosophy, and curriculum of entrepreneurs. In a modern world, digital entrepreneurship encompasses everything new and distinct about entrepreneurship, including:

- New ways of locating customers for entrepreneurial ventures
- Innovative ways of designing and offering products and services
- Unconventional ways of generating revenue and reducing cost
- Identification of fresh opportunities to collaborate with platforms and partners
- New sources of opportunity, risk, and competitive advantage

Digital entrepreneurship opens up new opportunities on a realistic basis for someone dreaming about being an entrepreneur. Some possibilities are more technical, but many others are within reach for someone who learns the fundamental skills of digital entrepreneurship. Such specific skills include looking online for potential clients, prototyping new business concepts, and improving data-based business ideas. Digital entrepreneurship is all about new ways of thinking about entrepreneurship itself and learning new technological skills, which is another way of suggesting that it introduces new entrepreneurship theories. New questions about the policy, chance, and risk are opened up by digital entrepreneurship. Digital entrepreneurship unlocks new opportunities in terms of education to train the future generation of entrepreneurs. 'Doing it' is the perfect way to practice entrepreneurship and draw on the learning. In the normal world, beginning the latest company or releasing a new product is expensive and dangerous for beginners. Not only does the modern world reduce the hurdles to beginning something new, but it provides a range of routes to growth. Educationally, it's such a different environment from case studies, simulations, and business plans. There is also controversy over the precise concept of digital entrepreneurship, partly because it is early and partly because it is changing. What is fresh in digital entrepreneurship can change over time as digital technology progresses. Maybe one day, any business projects will be born digital,' and digital entrepreneurship will cease to exist as a separate topic. However, today, there is a strong need to help educate entrepreneurs for the modern world and offer a new route to entrepreneurship to more individuals.

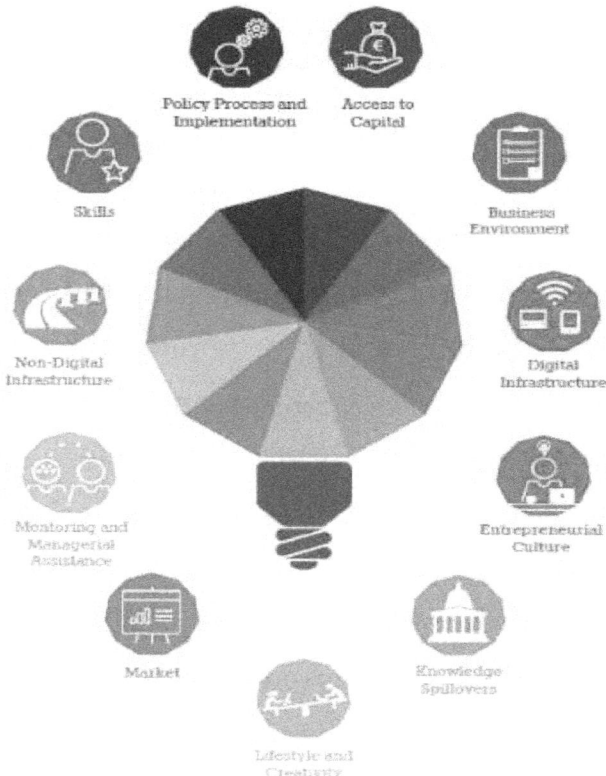

Simple Types of Digital Business Ideas

Digital marketers don't have a good sense of what is possible at the very beginning. It is advised that they begin with one of five basic forms to help beginners conceive of new digital business ideas:

A business offering knowledge on every specialized topic

It is possible to raise revenue through advertising, referrals, sponsorship, or merchandise

A neighborhood enterprise, hosting a vibrant and helpful discussion on every specialized topic

The sales opportunities are close to the industry of information

An online marketplace that markets goods or services

The objects may be tangible or digital

A matchmaker corporation that puts together two sets of individuals. For instance, a product or service provider (for instance, prospective babysitters) and another group who will need their services are always one group (parents looking for a babysitter). Advertising income is a probability, but with good matches, a transaction fee may also be received.

A promotional organization that draws online clients to a market that already exists

A possible revenue stream here, or advertising, is fees per client referral

An ideal new business plan can be impossible to come up with right from the start, but everyone will easily develop a realistic idea among these five options. As long as they can conceive of a subject that could attract at least a few hundred other individuals, a product or service they want to market, groups of individuals that may support each other, or some small company who could use some promotional assistance, digital entrepreneurs will launch their journey from the beginning. These five basic forms often make it easy for a digital business concept to be shared. In this case, a new business concept is:

A content provider on [your subject]

A [your subject] neighborhood business

An online shop that sells [your product or service]

A matchmaking firm that connects [service providers/group A] to [service users/group B]

The promotion of an online business [a local business]

The options are nearly infinite, and they are still evolving

Digital Entrepreneurship in the face of the Pandemic

Small firms and start-ups have been struck hardest by the recent pandemic than any other area of the economy. To survive a disaster, small firms usually have few resources. Usually, small companies still have little background in the new world of becoming creative, which is now one of their best choices for weathering the storm. In this moment of recession, a variety of digital practices can be considered by small companies. The typical guidance involves applying for federal support, staying in contact with online buyers, and beginning existing products' sales using e-commerce. These are all positive moves, but studies on digital entrepreneurship suggest some additional solutions. For small companies and start-ups, here are three extra fields of digital opportunity.

New models for doing business

It's a smart idea to learn ways to market your current goods online but think about marketing your experience as a new online service. Many families have at least one person with increased time to develop new things or with an immediate need to discover new, more customized ways to entertain themselves. Another option is to offer digital products, such as online classes or digital how-to guides, depending on your expertise. However, digital entrepreneurship helps you pursue brand new areas of operation and offer similar new goods and services. The opportunity to pursue innovative business ideas at little or low cost is a major benefit of digital entrepreneurship. Your new digital company, for instance, may provide useful knowledge that lets customers make other buying choices. During this recession, internet traffic and investment are up and catch these emerging internet traffic sources' attention. Advertisers and marketers are involved and can pay for quality customer leads. Display advertisements, performance advertising, sponsorships, and commission fees from affiliate marketing transactions are new revenue possibilities. Another new potential for digital business is to become a matchmaker, connect individuals who need an online product or service with someone who can better provide it, and charge a purchase fee or percentage. What types of people do you meet already? During this crisis, what are their special needs? And where can you refer them to for assistance? Many of the world's major digital matchmakers, Airbnbs and Ubers, would need to be temporarily replaced by more local alternatives that fit local conditions and will be able to handle local constraints as they evolve.

Perfect the digital business process

An easy way to think about digital business is to see it as an ABC method with three steps: acquisition, behavior, and conversion. The acquisition adds new buyers through social media campaigns, search results, email, search, or social advertisement, among many other platforms to the digital sector. Behavior is what tourists do to fulfill their needs and help them reach their goals through their digital presence. Conversion is the task that each of your guests would like to do, whether it's finishing order, clicking on advertisements, calling for an appointment, or installing a menu. In each of these three critical regions, this problem is an incentive for the organization to develop its capability. Now is a perfect time to create digital marketing campaigns for the acquisition of consumers. When they are ready to buy again, this will make buyers and opportunities ready for it. By enhancing the digital consumer experience, behavior can be changed. To see which ones are more popular, improve interaction, try new features, new content, and new ways to organize and manage your online presence. Your friend, here is the analytics data supplied by your digital company. An integral digital business capability is to turn tourists into future or real customers. Use the time to try new calls to action. It would help if you also used this opportunity to tell clients to do something that would improve their engagement. Practice getting the guests to do easier things such as likes, comments, and shares. Then intensify the participation by signing up for updates and discounts, uploading their material, or scheduling a future appointment. Don't fail to remember how they all come together when you practice each of the digital business ABCs. With promises that can't be met or ambitions that you can't meet, it's easy to have new tourists. Acquire the right visitors who are happy and will convert.

Start experimenting

The freedom to innovate continuously is a key advantage of digital entrepreneurship. There are several fresh ideas to try in each part of the ABC process. Get familiar with the analytics data, which will be from Google Analytics for most digital entrepreneurs. It will provide you with reliable input on what works and what doesn't. It is still being practiced by major corporations, conducting hundreds or thousands of tests on their clients every day. If they continue to remain competitive, small firms would need to develop the skills of digital experimentation. Fortunately, the benefit of emerging start-ups is that they can hop on emerging developments that are not yet big enough to interest the big players. A crisis scenario is a hotbed of emerging developments in the quest, new hashtags, new memes, and new points for the conversation to be taken advantage of. Once digital marketers discover innovative business concepts that work with their first 100 to 1,000 visitors, it is fairly inexpensive and easy to scale up such ideas when trends take off. Be on the lookout for new 'nano trends' as these developments play out, and be ready to expand.

CHAPTER 4: The Best Business

It doesn't need to require a big investment to start a profitable company. You can start a company without spending much capital, or even purchasing inventory, with a great business concept and the right resources. Adapting to a growing economy requires finding new, smart ways to fulfill clients' needs. To find the answer to the following important questions, you have to analyze the market:

What sorts of goods or services will fulfill the new consumer demands?

As an entrepreneur, how can your skills better fulfill those demands?

Any of the money-making, small business ideas that need very little investment are provided below.

4.1 Start your own online Dropshipper business

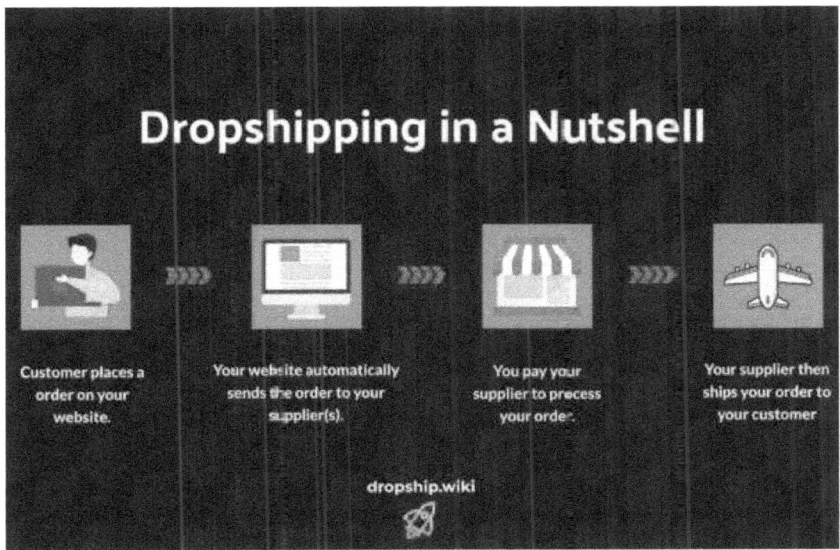

To sell online, you do not need to store inventory or spend a lot of money. You escape the expense of producing goods, handling inventory, and exporting with the dropshipping business by working with third-party vendors that do it all for you.

How it works

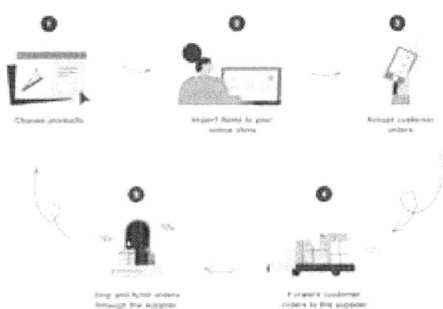

Dropshipping is a retail fulfillment technique where a retailer does not hold the items in storage that it offers. Instead, when a store sells a product using the dropshipping model, it orders the product from a third party and directly sends it to the consumer. As a consequence, the seller doesn't have to handle the items personally. The main contrast between dropshipping and the traditional retail model is that no product is held or controlled by the selling trader. Instead, to execute orders, the seller purchases inventory if appropriate from a third party, typically a wholesaler or retailer. You should start advertising your company using digital marketing tools to drive customers to your site once you're finished setting up your online store, and your site goes live. You'll get an order notice each time they make a transaction. They will complete it after the order is delivered to the supplier. You've just become the manager of your own e-commerce company. To get started with your dropshipping business, link your Wix account with Modalyst or Spocket. You can sell all kinds of great goods at your set prices after procuring products from millions of reliable suppliers. Just try to strike a balance with each sale between competitive prices and how much you earn.

Choose products to sell

You may need to select dropshipping items to sell before you launch your online business. Take the time for clarification of your brand and vision. To figure out what individuals are buying, do some market research. Before selling them in your store, determine the future demand, price, and profit margin of items. For an online shop, you will thrive by finding a way to stand out. Explore specialty items to source and market, and by offering a range, aim to stop placing all the eggs in one bowl. That said, to make your online store easier to browse, aim to organize your items into collections. Keep out of markets that are still saturated with stores. Take the time to set up marketing and advertising efforts to save you time and improve your revenue eventually.

Example: Trending work from home products

Think of what customers do at home to select the right business to establish with little investment. With equipment for living room workouts, open your online fitness shop. Open an adorable store selling puppy items for professionals working from home, such as quiet pet toys. It's all about feeling at ease in your home setting during COVID-19. It is why items such as sweatshirts, leggings, hoodies, slippers, and socks selling out everywhere. The athleisure trend has a moment. While people do not dress up at home as much, with cute pajama sets or multi-use makeup for a simple beauty routine, they may also look for ways to feel and look healthy. Your customers can also opt for at-the-home beauty items, such as grooming accessories or nail kits, with salons now less available.

As remote employees and students set up shop at home, home office products are also common. You have to dream of tech devices such as lap desks, laptop stands, desk organizers, keyboards, or home storage. The market has also spiked for ergonomic desk chairs that help posture and back alignment or convenient seat cushions. But not all of this is work and no play. As consumers search for new recreation ideas, gaming items have also become popular. As people look for things to do, at-home leisure products, such as game boards, trivia, or knitting equipment, sell well. Shoppers must spend more time cooking at home with restaurants closed. It suggests a spike in sales of kitchenware as well as online food and beverage items. Parents also need childcare and work-life to be tackled. So, consider adding quiet toys and play spaces to your dropshipping company, like the car park mats. Shoppers also like to video chat or watch Netflix with friends without holding their laptops all the time. In the dropshipping shop, try offering bedside mounts and table mounts.

Promote your online store

When you introduce items, it's time for your shop to be advertised. It Is where a strong approach for e-commerce marketing comes into play. Allow the best of the business software for the e-commerce website. Automate your email marketing promotions and client outreach to save time. Advertise your dropshipping business on Facebook and Instagram with paid campaigns. Work with influencers to support your brands and advertise them to their followers if it's important to your company. In promoting your online dropshipping business, your SEO strategy will also play a crucial role. It suggests the development of high-quality advertising and low-budget ads to improve the search engine results' exposure. Increase the visibility of your website with keyword optimization, for example. Let's presume you're selling home clothing for comfortable work. If you include the phrases "luxury comfort wear," "work from home," or "athleisure clothing" in your web copy, when people search for those keywords, you will have a better chance of ranking on Google.

Get creative with branded products designed by you

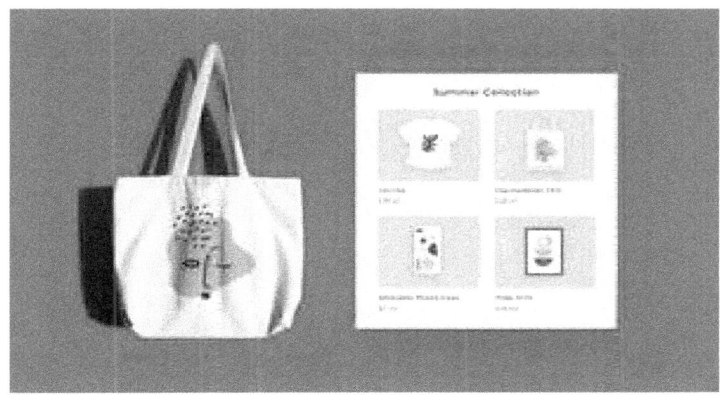

Now, let's take one step further with dropshipping. By linking Printful or Printify to your online shop, you add a personal touch with print on demand. You partner with print-on-demand businesses supplying the inventory, just like with dropshipping. Choose any customizable merchandise and introduce your creative touch, from t-shirts to phone cases, bags, and more. Go ahead and design graphics, quotations, or images to be printed on the chosen items. Start by choosing from thousands of different products to customize your online store and sell your designs. Start a business with funny quotes on a t-shirt. Add photos of your cat to Novelty Socks. Your logo or designs that match your brand create stickers—another cool option: selling goods made by you with original artwork. Yet, to market exclusive designs, you should not have to be a graphic artist. Hire and collaborate with freelance artists to create unique art for your products that are printed on-demand. You will distribute to over 90 places internationally when you receive an order. Forward your orders while managing everything from your Wix dashboard to your chosen supplier. Only think about it; shoppers would rock all over the world your exclusive creations.

Create digital video content

Now that individuals spend more time at home, by taking on new hobbies or returning to old ones, they're looking for ways to keep themselves occupied. Do you work in an industry, such as fitness, restaurants, or education, traditionally requires face-to-face interaction? Use this opportunity to create digital instruction videos, such as cooking demonstrations, workout routines, and more streamed online by people. The shutdown of schools and daycare services in 2021 means that parents have to spend a lot more time with their little ones at home. Moms and dads are searching for ways to keep their children busy, engaged, and learning. So if you are at home and temporarily out of a job, how can you apply your experience to satisfy this market demand? Especially now, family-friendly activities are always trendy. Get ahead of the competition by selling children-friendly video content. Create exercise videos for children if you're a fitness trainer. Promote the use of child-friendly content, such as workouts or classes for baby yoga. To help parents home-school their children, post daily lessons online. With your children, you can even create an entertaining cooking show. With digital video content, there are distinct pricing models to earn money. To give customers full access to exclusive content, you may charge a monthly channel subscription. You can monetize your content based on the number of viewers if you work with video hosting platforms like YouTube. Selling or renting your videos is another option. Over a 24-48-hour cycle, viewers may download the video or watch it on your site. To give clients an idea of your product and nudge them to make a purchase, consider offering some of your content for free. Zoom, Vimeo, and YouTube can also host live streaming or webinars.

Comprehend the Supply Chain of Dropshipping

Supply chain's some fancy word that defines the journey a commodity takes to move from creation through manufacture and eventually into a customer's hands. If we are talking about suppliers of hard core chains gurus, they would insist that the supply chain stretches all towards mining products to make an object (like oil & rubber). But it's a bit intense. We do not need to be quite so specific. The three most important participants in the dropshipping supply chain must simply be understood: wholesalers, manufacturers, & retailers.

Manufacturers

Manufacturers produce the commodity, & most don't sell directly to the public. They sell bulks to wholesalers & dealers instead. The easiest way to buy goods for resale is to buy straight from the manufacturer, but most of them have minimum purchasing standards you'll desire to follow. When shipping them to consumers, you'll still need to store & re-ship goods. It's also cheaper to buy from the wholesaler for these purposes directly.

Wholesalers

Wholesalers purchase products from manufacturers in bulk, mark them up marginally and then market them to the retailers to sell them to the public. They're normally much smaller than those needed by a vendor if they have buying minimums. Wholesalers normally store goods from thousands of producers, if not a hundred, and prefer to work in a single field or drop shipping niche. Many operators are exclusively wholesalers. It means that they only sell to retailers & not direct to the general public.

Retailers

the retailer is anyone who sells the products directly to the public after adding his margin. If you are running a business that fulfills your orders through dropshipping suppliers, you are a retailer.

Dropshipping is a service, not a role

You will find that "drop shipper" is not one of the supply chain players. Each of the three will operate as drop shippers - manufacturer, wholesaler, and retailer. If the manufacturer is prepared to supply its supplies directly to your consumer, it's "dropshipping" for your sake. Similarly, a supermarket retailer will offer drop ship, but its price would not be as favorable as a wholesaler because the manufacturer does not buy it directly. It doesn't mean you're having bulk rates simply because someone declares to be a "drop shipper." It means that, for your sake, the company would ship goods. You desire to ensure that you deal exclusively with a reputable manufacturer or wholesaler to get the best prices.

The order process

Let us observe how the drop shipped order is processed so that you have understood the players involved. We would follow the order put with a theoretical shop, an online seller Phone Outlet, specializing in smartphone accessories, to demonstrate. Phone Outlet dropships all its items directly from the wholesaler that we will call Wholesale Accessories. Here's a sample of what the whole ordering process could look like:

Customer Places Order With Phone Outlet

Allen requires a case for the new smartphone and places an order through the Phone Outlet online store. A few things happen once an order has been approved:

Phone Outlet & Mr. Allen would receive an email of confirmation (likely alike) of new orders which store software automatically generates.

During the checkout process, the payment of Mr. Allen is captured and automatically placed into the bank account of Phone Outlet.

Phone Accessory Outlet Places the Order With Its Supplier

The step is generally as artless as sending the confirmation of an email order to a sales representative at Wholesale Accessories by Phone Outlet. Wholesale Accessories has a credit card from Phone Outlet on file & will charge it for wholesale goods, including handling fees or shipping. Some sophisticated drop shippers will support XML Automatic (a normal format for stock files) orders uploading or the ability to place orders manually online. Still, email is the most common method to place orders with dropshipping vendors because it is universal & easier to use.

Wholesale accessories ships the order

If items in the stock and wholesaler have positively charged the Phone Outlet card, the order will be boxed up and shipped directly to the customer by Wholesale Accessories. Although shipments come from the Wholesale Accessories, the name & address of the Phone Outlet would appear on the label of the return address, and the logo would appear on the invoice & packing slip. Wholesale Accessories would then email invoice & tracking numbers to the Phone Outlet once the shipment has been finalized.

Turnaround time is often quicker than you would think on dropshipped orders. In a few hours, most feature suppliers would be capable of getting the order outdoor, allowing merchants to publicize shipping on the same day when they use drop shipping suppliers.

Phone outlet alerts the customer of shipment

When this tracking number's collected, Phone Outlet gives the customer tracking information, potentially using an email interface built into the online store interface. The order and delivery process is complete with the order delivered, the invoice received, and a customer told. The benefit (or loss) of Phone Outlet is the contrast between what this costs Mr. Allen & what this paid for wholesale accessories.

Dropshippers are invisible

The drop shipper is invisible to the end buyer, despite its vital position in the ordering & fulfillment process. Just the Phone Outlet return address & signature would be on the shipment when the package is received. If Mr. Allen obtains the wrong case, he will call Phone Outlet, who would work with Wholesale Accessories behind scenes and get the right item shipped out. To the ultimate buyer, the wholesaler does not exist. Stocking and shipping dropshipping products is the sole responsibility. The merchant is responsible for all else—website creation, marketing, customer support.

4.2 How to Find and Work with Reliable Dropshipping Suppliers

One of the most popular questions ambitious entrepreneurs pose is: What is my e-commerce store's best dropshipping supplier? Supplier directory for dropshipping is a distributor database grouped by niche, market, or commodity. Many of the directories employ a few scanning mechanisms to ensure that legitimate wholesalers are suppliers listed. Many are managed by for-the profit corporations who charge a fee to use their directories. While membership folders, particularly for brainstorming the ideas, may be useful, they're by no means essential. If you already know the commodity or drop shipping niche that you need to sell, you must locate the big suppliers in the market with a little bit of searching & the techniques mentioned above. Plus, you once start dropshipping company, unless you want to locate suppliers for the other things, you would probably not need to revisit the directory. That said, the supplier directory is an easy way to scan for or/and browse a vast range of suppliers in 1 location easily and is useful for brainstorming ideas for marketing goods or entering niches. If you are short of time and ready to spend cash, a helpful tool may be supplier directories. There is a range of different suppliers and businesses for dropshipping.

Best dropshipping suppliers

CJdropshipping

Oberlo

CROV

DropnShop

Supplymedirect

Modalyst

To make this easier to select best drop shipping companies for specific needs, we will focus on the following factor:

Location and shipping options

So, Where do the supplier's locations exist? How much time is consumed in producing the item after the customer has put orders?

Product types

Which kinds of products they dropship?

Recommended for

And Is the particular suppliers suited for experienced or beginner dropshippers?

Oberlo

Shopify. The Oberlo is dropshipping the platform, making it easier to find AliExpress items to sell in the Shopify store. It is the best online drop shipping supplier directory for Shopify. The platform provides over 30 thirty of the latest dropshipping goods from vendors across the globe in 60 plus niche categories. Oberlo has free registration, beginning at 29.9 dollars a month for paid plans.

Location & shipping options

In different places around the world, Oberlo links you with suppliers. Usually, each includes many delivery solutions for the clients to send products. On each commodity page in the Oberlo app, you will find what delivery methods the supplier uses. the Popular shipping method includes:

China Post. Affordable / Free shipping expenses. Delivery could take 20 to 50 days.

AliExpress Shipping. Affordable costs of shipping. Delivery can take up to 15 days.

ePacket. Affordable / Free shipping expenses. Delivery could take 15 to 30 days.

DHL/UPS/FedEx. Express the shipping expenses. Delivery could take between five to fifteen days.

Product types

So You may find anything that includes bracelets, antiques, car parts, wedding supplies, sunglasses, furniture, and much more.

Recommended for

It's recommended for the beginner & veteran drop shipper.

CJDropshipping

With fast delivery, it is the best dropshipping service. CJDropshipping is a marketplace that allows retailers to scale up the drop shipping business affordably. You can conveniently import goods directly from 1688 and Taobao marketplaces into the Shopify store, usually at a price lesser than on AliExpress. Along with other dropshipping applications like Oberlo, it's also a free Shopify application that you could add to the store.

Location & shipping options

To perform processing on the same-day for the store, CJDropshipping uses US-based warehouses. UPS, USPS, DHL, & FedEx work with it.

The shipping line known as CJPacket will bring goods to the US in 7 to twelve days if you are shipping from China.

Product types

Independent designers & owners of small businesses in China are home to the 1668 and Taobao marketplaces. Via CJDropshipping, there are 100s of millions of listings you may browse, & products vary from mainstream goods to difficult-to-find items & even the virtual product. If the CJDropshipping app does not have a product, you can upload a request & CJDropshipping would list this once the best source is identified.

Recommended for

The retailer who needs a 1-stop location for all the things drop shipping, including inventory procurement, order preparation, distribution, and fast shipping to United States, is highly recommended.

SupplyMeDirect

It is the strongest dropshipping provider for the UK, US, & European markets for private labels. SupplyMeDirect is a wholesale provider that supports the size of dropshipping business. The app provides private labeling & secure sourcing. It's a free Shopify application that you could contact twenty-four 7, supported by dedicated support staff.

Location & shipping options

The SupplyMeDirect is different. The reason is that nearly 60 percent of the stock resides in the warehouses established in the United States, the UK, Canada, & Europe. It makes shipping reliable and fast. The shipping has an average time of delivery of 4 to 7 days.

Product types

Any product from apparel to kitchenware, the toys to the accessories, & more

Recommended for

It is best for the drop shippers who intend to sell in the whole world & want fast shipping.

CROV

For the multi-channel vendors, it is the strongest dropshipping provider. CROV links retailers from vetted lists of US vendors to a wide variety of items. It is yet another free-of-cost Shopify app to populate the store with products and automate orders.

Location & shipping options

In the 42 countries, shipping is available. Costs rely on vendors & their shipping processes, which can be found in a directory on every product detail page. To ship the domestic orders quicker, CROV has a US warehouse.

Product types

It offers extra than 35 thousand products in more than 20 other trending categories from the selected suppliers.

Recommended for

It is the best for eCommerce sellers. Especially for those who need to sell different products on Amazon, Shopify, & eBay.

Modalyst

It is the greatest supplier of dropshipping high-tickets for US apparel. For online retailers, Modalyst is an automatic dropshipping program. It is known for delivering items that customers would enjoy from the brand names such as DSquare, Calvin Klein, Dolce, and Gabbana, & other famous brands. For any target demographic, Modalyst often features a curated collection of independent & trendy brands. The website has an official API collaboration with AliExpress Dropshipping, allowing you to access the millions of items with a Google Chrome plugin to connect to your shop with one click.

Location & shipping options

The Modalyst has the own marketplace of US manufacturers and products that can offer domestic orders free of charge between six to eight days. Also available are UK dropshipping vendors & Australian drop shippers. Businesses, except countries in South America and Africa, will ship to more than 80 countries in the world

Product types

It generally emphasizes premium and fashionable products. Modalyst is part of the Booster Program of AliExpress also, offering an infinite catalog of items for drop shippers to browse.

Recommended for

It is recommended for users of Shopify who want their shops to add exclusive items. You will also market goods using Modalysts Private Label Software with your branding. You will take advantage of any of the luxury brands and vendors that Modalysts has to sell if you chose the Pro plan.

dropship

It is the best source of dropships for French goods. DropnShop is a dropshipping program for Shopify that provides online sales of French goods. It offers inventory from the top factories of French. It takes the requests from e-commerce partners to diversify product catalog and expand your business due to partnerships with thousands of producers. There's an availability-free plan.

Location & shipping information

To have worldwide delivery at a decent rate, DropnShop partners with numerous suppliers. Every product has different shipping information, but you may find anything you require to know on the product detail page of the app.

Product types

Would you like to sell France's best cosmetics products in your shop? With DropnShop, you may. The supplier also sells 1000s of SKUs, all 100 percent manufactured in France, across several categories, from children's toys to the hair & products of skincare.

Recommended for

It is the best for eCommerce stores. It is best, especially for those who desire to add the French product to the catalog.

Let us learn to find dropshipping suppliers

Suppliers are not always made equal, like most things in life. It is also more important to ensure that you are dealing with top-notch players in the dropshipping community. The supplier is a vital part of the dropshipping fulfillment operation.

Before you contact suppliers

Okay, so you've discovered a range of good suppliers & are prepared to go forward—great! Yet you would want to get all ducks in a row before you start approaching businesses.

It would help if you were legal

we discussed earlier, before authorizing you to register for some account, most amazing wholesalers would need confirmation that you are a legal entity. Most wholesalers report their prices to licensed consumers, but you will need to be legally authorized before seeing the type of pricing you will receive. Before contacting vendors, make sure you're lawfully integrated.

Don't be afraid of the phone

One of the strongest worries people have is picking up phone & making the call when it comes to vendors. It is a paralyzing prospect for many. For such problems, you may be capable of sending texts, but you'll have to pick the phone up more frequently than not to get the answers you need. The good news's that this isn't as terrifying as you would imagine. Suppliers, including novice entrepreneurs, are used to having the people calling them. You're going to get someone to answer questions who's polite and happier. Here's a trick to motivate you: just type your questions down in advance. When you have a list of already written questions for asking, it is surprising how easy it's to make the call. Great vendors for dropshipping tends to have most of the following six characteristics:

Expert staff and industry focus

There are knowledgeable distribution agents from top-notch manufacturers who truly know the market and the product lines. It's invaluable to contact a representative with concerns, especially if you're starting a store in a niche you're not too familiar with anything.

Dedicated support representatives

individual sales agent responsible for taking good care of yourself & any concerns you have should assign you to quality drop shippers. Problems take even longer to fix because we generally must nag the people to take care of a crisis. Getting a single interaction with a supplier allows you to locate the entity responsible for fixing your problems which is very valuable.

Invest in technology

When there are many great suppliers with obsolete websites, suppliers that know the advantages of technology and spend extensively in it are typically a joy to deal with them. For online retailers, features like an inventory of real-time, a detailed online catalog, personalized data feeds & online searchable history of orders are pure pleasure & may help streamline the activities.

Can take orders via email

it may seem like a small challenge, but have to call in each order or put it manually on a website makes handling orders even more time-consuming.

Centrally located

It's helpful to use a centrally placed drop shipper in a big country like the United States since shipments can cover more than 90percent of the country within 2-3 business days. It may take an additional week for shipments to be delivered around the country where a retailer is based on one coast. Centrally placed vendors allow guaranteeing quicker turnaround times reliably, theoretically saving you cash on shipping costs.

Organized and efficient

few vendors have qualified personnel and outstanding processes that contribute to effective and often error-less fulfillment. Every 4th order will be botched by others & make you need to rip the hair out. But without ever using it, its impossible to tell how a professional supplier is.

While it cannot give you the full picture, it will give you a better sense of how suppliers perform by placing a few small test orders. You can see:

How to order process is done

How rapidly things ship out

And How fast this follows with monitoring details and invoice

quality of package when the product arrives

It is important to learn how to distinguish between genuine suppliers of wholesale & retail stores acting as wholesale suppliers when looking for suppliers. A real wholesaler buys straight from the producer & will usually offer you even better prices.

How to spot fake dropshipping companies

You will come across a significant number of " fake" wholesalers based on where you're looking. Unfortunately, historically, legal wholesalers are bad at selling and appear to be more difficult to find. It results in non-genuine wholesalers showing more often in searches, usually only intermediaries, so you'll need to be careful. Following dropshipping tips would help you decide whether it is a legal wholesale supplier.

They want ongoing fees

Real wholesalers don't charge their clients monthly fees for the luxury of doing a business & buying from them. It's usually not legitimate if a retailer asks for a monthly subscription or a service fee. It's necessary to distinguish between the suppliers and directories of suppliers here. Supplier directories are bulk supplier directories grouped by commodity categories or sector & screened to ensure suppliers' authenticity. Many directories, either 1-time or continuous, can charge a fee, but you do not take it as an indication that the directory itself's unlawful.

They sell to the public

You would need to register for a wholesale account to get real wholesale rates, demonstrate you are a legal entity, and be accepted before making your first order. So Any wholesale seller selling goods at "wholesale" to the general public is the only retailer offering the items at inflated rates. However, here are a few legal dropshipping charges that you would possibly encounter:

Per-order fees

Depending on the size and complexity of the goods being dispatched, certain drop shippers would charge a dropshipping fee per shipment that can vary from 2-5 dollars or more. As the prices of packaging and delivering individual order is much greater than shipping bulk order, this is common in the industry.

Minimum order sizes

There would be a minimum beginning order size for certain wholesalers, which is the lowest sum you may have to buy for your 1st order. They perform this to weed out window shopping vendors with questions & minor orders that will not translate into real sales and will waste their resources. If you're dropshipping, some problems may be caused. For starters, what would you might do if you have a minimum order of $500 from a supplier, but your mean order size takes about $100? Only for the privilege of making a dropshipping account do you not want to pre-order $500 of the stuff. It's best to make an offer to pay the seller $500 in advance, in this case, to create a loan with them to apply for the drop shipping orders. It helps you fulfill the retailer's minimum purchase obligation (as you are committed to buying a product at least 500 dollars in product) without having to position a single big order without accompanying any customer requests.

Tips for working with dropshipping wholesalers

It's time to start looking for vendors now you can detect a scam from the actual deal! There are a variety of different techniques that you may use, some more successful than others. In order of usefulness and choice, the ways below are enlisted, with the preferred methods enlisted first.

Contact the manufacturer

It may be the ideal way for legal bulk vendors to be conveniently identified. Contact the manufacturer to inquire about their wholesale dealers' list if you know the product(s) you intend to dropship. To observe if they dropship and ask about setting an account up, you may then email these wholesalers. Because most wholesalers carry goods from several manufacturers within the niche, you are pursuing, and this strategy would permit you to source a range of items easily. You'll easily be able to find the leading wholesalers in that market after making few calls to leading producers in some niche.

Use Oberlo

Oberlo helps you quickly import goods straight into the Shopify store from vendors and directly send them to your consumers, all in some clicks.

Features

Products can be imported from suppliers

Product customization

Orders are fulfilled automatically

Inventory & price automatic updates

Pricing automation

Search using Google

You may use Google to fetch high-quality suppliers. It is quite obvious, yet there are some factors to keep in mind:

You have to search extensively

Wholesales are not good at marketing & promotion. Furthermore, they aren't going to cover the top search results related to "wholesale suppliers for some product X." You will have to do all the research yourself.

Don't judge by their website

Wholesales are now infamous for making '90s-style websites. Although a quality site can suggest a successful supplier in some instances, many legal wholesalers have cringe-worthy website homepages. Don't let you get turned off by the bad design.

Attend a trade show

trade show helps you to engage in a niche with all key manufacturers & wholesalers. It's a perfect method to make friends, all in one place, and research the commodities and suppliers. It only applies if the niche &/or product has already been chosen, and it is not possible for everybody. But it's a perfect method to know vendors and the suppliers in the region if you have the time and resources to participate.

Ways to pay dropshipping suppliers and companies

A large number of suppliers shall accept payments in 1 of 2 ways:

Credit card

Many suppliers will ask you to make the payment by credit card as you're starting. Paying with credit cards is always the better choice after you've developed a flourishing business. Not only are they easy (no requirement to constantly write checks), but lots of loyalty frequent flier/ points miles can be racked up. You will rack up a high number of sales with your credit card without requiring to pay any real out-of-the-pocket costs when you are purchasing a product for a client who has already paid for it on your website.

Net terms

"Net terms" on invoices are the most typical method to pay the suppliers. It assumes that you have certain days for paying the retailer with the items you have ordered. So if you're on the "net 30" term, you have exactly 30 days to pay the supplier for the items from the purchase date you ordered by bank draw or check. Usually, before providing net payment terms, a supplier would make you have credit references, so it's lending you money. It is a normal procedure, but if you have to provide any documentation while paying on net terms, do not be alarmed.

Usually, before providing net payment terms, a supplier would make you have credit references, so it's lending you the money. It's a normal procedure, but if you need to provide any documentation while paying on the net terms, do not be alarmed.Bottom of Form

Top of Form

Bottom of Form

FAQs about dropshipping suppliers

Given below are some of the frequently asked questions, along with answers about the dropshipping suppliers.

How do I find dropshipping suppliers?

On directory vetted such as Oberlo, you can find dropshipping suppliers, colleagues' suggestions, or look the suppliers for the products for brands you like. You may also find several excellent alternatives with some research work.

What are the best dropshipping suppliers in 2021?

Some top suppliers for dropshipping are Worldwide Labels, Doba, SaleHoo, AliExpress, Alibaba, Wholesale Central, & CDS.

Is dropshipping still profitable in 2021?

In 2021, dropshipping also represents a viable market opportunity. Since you don't need to spend on the inventory or incur holding expenses, it's a sustainable business model.

Which platform is best for dropshipping?

Combined with the Oberlo, Shopify allows for a streamlined setup for dropshipping. On Oberlo, you can check for vendors and make items available on the branded Shopify website for sale. You make the sales, & your drop shipping supplier will do the rest.

Common questions about dropshipping

We have compiled a list of questions that could be posed by anyone planning to start a new drop shipper business.

How much do I need to invest in starting dropshipping?

While it is difficult to predict exact prices for any individual company, to get started, there are few things on which each drop shipping company would need to be spending money. Here's a short rundown of the critical expenditures.

Online store

Estimated price: ~29 dollars per month

To establish & host an online shop, you'll need to find an e-commerce site. We suggest launching a shop at Shopify. You will be capable of syncing source items with Oberlo marketplace conveniently, and you will get access to a full range of themes & free branding software so that you can quickly get your company up & running.

Domain name

Estimated price: $5 to 20 per year

Without the domain name, it's difficult to develop trust with clients. Although there is a range of top-leveled domains available (example,

example. co example. shop), if one is available, we recommend searching for the .com which suits the brand.

Test orders

Estimated price: Varies

While dropshipping helps you to have limited interference in managing your total product catalog, that you can set aside, also little of the time, cash to test the items you want to sell. You threaten listing products with too many flaws or faults if you don't, which will lead to disappointed consumers and a lot of the time wasted coping with refunds.

Online advertising

Estimated price: the Scales with the business; It is recommended to start budgeting with a minimum of $500

Each e-commerce organization must look for ways of reducing the average cost of acquiring a client across organic networks such as SEO, content marketing, & word of mouth. But advertising is typically an important medium for many product-based firms to start every company. Search engine marketing (the SEM), displays advertising, social media advertising, and smartphone ads are among the most common channels.

How do drop shippers make money?

Dropshipping businesses act like product curators, choosing the best dropshipping products for market to the customers; remember that marketing costs you incur, into both time & money, help the potential customers find, explain, & buy the right products. You will also have to include the cost of supporting customers whenever there is a product or a shipping problem. Last but not least is the original price for which the supplier sells a product. With all these prices to be accountable for, the dropshipping business mark up the individual products in exchange for the distribution. It's why the suppliers are okay with having drop shippers markets the products for those people—dropshipping stores also drive extra sales, which supplier would've missed out otherwise. it is good to find out how much this costs to "acquire" customer, & price the products with it in mind.

Is dropshipping a legitimate business?

Dropshipping is essentially a fulfillment model, one used with many global distributors, and is completely legitimate. Satisfying consumer needs and creating brands that resonate with the right demographic is also vital for long-term growth, as with any company. Owing to a misconception of how dropshipping works, this question generally occurs. The bulk of discount shops at which you shop are most likely not to sell items they directly make. Dropshipping takes the curated approach & converts it into an online company-fit distribution model. of course, you must do more simple things to operate your business lawfully. To guarantee that you are doing business lawfully in your country, find a lawyer who has specialized in these matters.

Benefits of dropshipping

For emerging entrepreneurs, dropshipping is a perfect business model to start with because it's accessible. You can easily test multiple business concepts with a small drawback with dropshipping, which helps you learn a lot about picking and selling in-demand goods. In

2021, dropshipping is still a viable market opportunity. Since you don't need to spend in inventory or incur holding expenses, it's a sustainable business model. Combined with Oberlo, Shopify allows for a streamlined setup for dropshipping. On Oberlo, you can check for vendors and make items available on your branded Shopify site for sale. You make purchases, and your drop shipping provider will do the rest.

Less capital is required

Stocking a warehouse takes a lot of money. By using dropshipping, you can eliminate the possibility of falling into debt to start your company. You can launch a dropshipping company with zero inventory instead of buying an extensive inventory and hoping it sells and start making money immediately. Perhaps the greatest bonus of dropshipping is that an e-commerce website can be opened without having to spend thousands of dollars in stock upfront. Traditionally, manufacturers have had to bind up large quantities of inventory with capital investments. For the dropshipping model, unless you have already made the sale and have been paid by the consumer, you do not have to buy a product. It is possible to start sourcing goods without substantial up-front inventory investments and begin a profitable dropshipping company with very little capital. And because you're not dedicated to selling, as in a typical retail company, there's less danger involved in launching a dropshipping shop without any inventory bought upfront.

Easy to get started

Managing an e-commerce business is much easier as you don't have to deal with physical products. With drop shipping, you won't have to worry about:

Warehouse cost and management

Handling returns and inbound shipments

Packing and shipping of your orders

Keeping track of inventory for accounting purposes

Perpetually ordering products

Continuously managing stock level

Low cost of inventory

If you own and warehouse stock, inventory is one of the biggest costs you would have. You can end up with old inventory, causing you to find ways to reduce your inventory, or you may end up with very little inventory, resulting in stockouts and missed sales. Dropshipping lets you escape these challenges and concentrate on increasing your client base and developing your brand.

Low Order Fulfillment Costs

Usually, order fulfillment requires you to store, organize, label, select and carry and ship your inventory. Dropshipping lets all of it be taken care of by a third party. In this arrangement, the sole job is to ensure that they receive customer requests. They will do all the rest.

Low overhead

Your operating rates are minimal because you don't have to do with buying inventory or maintaining a warehouse. In reality, many popular dropshipping stores are managed as home-based enterprises, needing nothing more to run than a laptop and a few recurring costs. These costs are likely to escalate as you expand, but they will still be low relative to those of conventional brick-and-mortar companies.

Flexible location

From just about anywhere with an internet connection, a drop shipping company can be managed. You can run and handle your company as long as you can effectively connect with vendors and clients.

A wide selection of products to sell

Without the limitations of a physical inventory and the associated costs, dropshipping allows you to rapidly, comfortably, and cheaply upgrade your inventory. You will instantly deliver it to your customers without waiting for it to arrive in your factory if you know that a product is doing well for another store or reseller. Without the risk of bringing old products, dropshipping helps you to try new products. You're paying just for what you offer. Since you don't have to pre-purchase the items you sell, you can show your future buyers various trending products. If suppliers store an item, you can list it for sale at no added cost at your online store.

Easier to test

Dropshipping is a valuable form of fulfillment for both the opening of a new store and for company owners looking to measure consumers' demand for additional types of items, such as shoes or whole new product ranges. Again, the primary advantage of dropshipping is the opportunity to list and likely sell goods before committing to purchasing a significant quantity of stock.

Easier to scale

For a typical retail organization, you would typically need to do three times as much work if you get three times the orders. By leveraging dropshipping vendors, suppliers will be responsible for most of the work to handle extra orders, helping you to improve with fewer growing pains and less gradual work. Sales growth can often bring extra labor, especially customer service, but companies that use dropshipping scale particularly well compared to conventional e-commerce companies

Conclusion

Digital entrepreneurship may be clearly described as entrepreneurial businesses which are carried through a digital medium. Most studies proved that entrepreneurship a crucial driver for economic development & also for the reduction of unemployment. I's really important to grasp all the principles relevant to entrepreneurship. For meeting market competition & achieve the business target, every entrepreneur must be up to date with changes that arise in the customer's tastes & desires and even in the market. It is often important to use certain new digital technology & softwares to connect with the consumers and increase quality demand. As today's environment is largely dependent on national & global technology, it is important to have the sector's technologies. In this way, digital entrepreneurship plays a critical role in enabling the entrepreneur to conduct all the tasks accurately and efficiently. Using software apps allows any entrepreneur to increase the market demand for his or her product & grow the business both technologically and traditionally. As the Information & communication technologies (ICT) skills are crucial elements of digital enterprise success, it's significant to learn how it allows people to improve their business so that you can use the same for creating your own successful business. It will allow any person who engages in the business to learn about digital entrepreneurship in the Present world, changing dramatically in all fields, particularly in information & communication technology (ICT). In this case, the exponential growth of emerging technology with new creative functionalities is changing competitive environment, modifying the general market strategies, systems, and the procedure. For example, on networked economy motorized by new technologies, many businesses or company is becoming tinier with just one person where the partnerships are evolving. Digital Innovative technologies, including big data, social media, and mobile & cloud platforms, are giving rise to new ways of collaborating, exploiting capital, service/product design, creation, and deployments over the open standards & collaborative technologies. They're, in turn, impacting the market activities through generating job opportunities. Like, Alibaba.com is digital technology that allowed millions of Chinese people to be entrepreneurs. It is also responsible for the creation of employment.

Even digital technologies generate vast job opportunities. They're creating several challenges also. Emerging technologies are modernizing the labor market. Several countries are facing several obstacles, such as Australia, to face economic competition. To face the obstacles and eliminate the barriers, countries are recommended for taking over digital entrepreneurship & achieve an acceptable role. Digital entrepreneurship increases jobs across ICTs like Facebook, social computing, mobile technology, and digital channels. Many firms began digital businesses by selling the products online to meet competition in the industry. As this becomes necessary, focusing on how a business venture must be started is rising with utmost significance. People who need to start a digital company should know the differences between digital versus conventional opportunities, downfalls, entrepreneurship, and digital entrepreneurship challenges. The people need a format or digital entrepreneurship system that consists all information about the new digital enterprise, including its features and objectives.

The 9+1 Best Home-Based Business Model of 2021

Find Out how Millennials Have Built Millionaire Businesses from Home with Soap and Candle Making, Natural Cosmetics and much more

By

Nespy Online Marketing

Table of Contents

Introduction	81
CHAPTER 1: The Nirma Washing Powder's Success Story	84
1.1 Invention of Nirma detergent?	85
1.2 Karsanbhai Patel's sale policy for Nirma detergent	87
1.3 Invest In Research and Development	88
1.4 No Higher Costs	89
1.5 Be Proactive in your approach as it is beneficial for the business	90
1.6 Provide Customers with 'Value for Money'	91
1.7 Define Your Segment	91
1.8 Focus on Building a Brand	92
1.9 Astutely Manage the Brand Wars	93
1.10 Diversify the Portfolio	95
1.11 Conclusion	96
1.12 What Karsanbhai Patel and Nirma detergent did for the Indian Economy	97
1.13 Karsanbhai Patel's ventures other than the Nirma detergent	97
CHAPTER 2: Start a Profitable Soap Making Business	99

2.1 What will you name your business? 104

2.2 Form a legal entity 104

2.3 Small Business Taxes 105

2.4 Open a business bank account & credit card 105

2.5 Open a business bank account 105

2.6 Get a business credit card 106

2.7 Obtain necessary permits and licenses 106

2.8 State & Local Business Licensing Requirements 106

2.9 Labor safety requirements 107

2.10 Certificate of Occupancy 107

2.11 Trademark & Copyright Protection 108

2.12 Get business insurance 108

2.13 Learn more about General Liability Insurance 108

2.14 Define your brand 109

2.15 Soap Making Plan 110

2.16 Soap selling process 118

2.17 Soap making supplies 119

2.18 Marketing area for soap 120

2.19 Total investment 120

2.20 Selling price — 121

2.21 Profit margin — 121

2.22 Precaution — 122

2.23 Risk — 122

2.24 Conclusion — 122

2.25 Advantage of starting a soap making business at home — 122

2.26 How Much Money Can You Make Making Soap? — 123

CHAPTER 3: Start a Profitable Candle Making Business — 125

3.1 Steps for starting a candle making business — 125

3.2 How much can you charge customers? — 129

3.3 Benefits of candle making business — 139

Conclusion — 141

Introduction

Karsanbhai Patel (Patel), the chemist at Mines and Geology Department of the Gujarat Government, produced synthetic powder of detergent phosphate-free in 1969 and began selling this locally. He priced the new yellow powder at 3.50rs per kg. It was at one time when Rs 15 was being charged for Hindustan Lever Limited (HLL) Surf. Soon, in Kishnapur (Gujarat), Patel's hometown, there was a big demand for Nirma. In 10x12 feet space in his home, he began preparing the formula. He had named powder after his daughter's name-Nirupama. On the way to the office by bicycle, about 15 kilometers away, Patel was able to sell around 15-20 packets a day. Thus, the new journey began. Hindustan Lever Limited (HLL) responded in a manner characteristic of many global corporations in the early 1970s, when washing powder Nirma was launched into the market of low-income. "That isn't our business," senior executives said of the new offering. "We don't have to be worried." However very soon, Hindustan Lever Limited (HLL) was persuaded by Nirma's performance in the detergent sector that this wanted to take a closer gaze at the less income market. Low-cost detergents & toilet soaps are almost synonymous with the brand name. Nirma, on the other hand, found that it would've to launch goods targeted at the higher end of the market to maintain the middle-class buyers as they moved up the market. For the luxury market, the firm introduced bathroom soaps. Analysts, on the other hand, claimed Nirma wouldn't be capable of duplicate its performance in the premium market. In the year 2000, the Nirma had a 15 percent share of the toilet soap market and a 30% share of the detergent market. Nirma's revenue for the year ended in March 2000 grew by 17 percent over the previous fiscal year, to 17.17rs. bn, backed by volume development and commissioning of backward integration projects. By 1985, in many areas of the world, washing powder Nirma became one of the most common detergent brands. Nirma was a global consumer company by 1999, with a wide variety of soaps, detergents, & personal care items. Nirma has brought in the latest technologies for the manufacturing facilities in six locations across India, in line with its ideology of delivering premium goods at the best possible costs. The success of Nirma in the intensely competitive market for soaps & detergents was due to its efforts to support the brand, which had been complemented by the sales scope & market penetration. The network of Nirma spread across the country, with over two million outlets of retail and 400 distributors. Nirma was able to reach out to even the smallest villages due to its vast network. Nirma spread to the markets overseas in 1999 after establishing itself in India. Via a joint venture called Commerces Overseas Limited, it made its first foray into Bangladesh. Within a year, the company had risen to the top of Bangladesh's detergent market. Other areas such as Middle East, Russia, China, Africa & additional Asian countries were also intended for the entry of the organization. Nirma became a 17 billion Rs company in 3 decades, beginning as a single-product single-man article of clothing in 1969. Under the umbrella name Nirma, the company had several production plants and a large product range. The mission of the organization to have "Better Product, Better Values and Better Living" added much to its growth. Nirma was able to outshine Hindustan Levers Limited (then HLL) and carve out a niche for oneself in the lower-ends of detergent & market toilet soap. HLL's Surf was the first to be used as a detergent powder in India in 1959. But by the 1970s, merely by making the product available at a reasonable price, Nirma led the demand for detergent powder. Nirma launched its Nirma Beauty soaps to the Indian toilet soap industry in 1990. Nirma had gained a 15% share of 530,000 tons per annum toilet soap industry by 1999, making it India's second-largest producer. Although it was way behind HLL's 65 percent share, the success of Nirma was impressive compared to Godrej, which had an 8 percent share. By 1999-2000, Nirma had already acquired a 38 percent share of India's detergent market of 2.4 million tonnes. For the same period, HLL's market share was 31%. In this book, we will study and analyze the case of Nirma and its rise to the top detergent companies of India. Besides, we will also give profitable ideas and options for starting a lucrative detergent soap, candle making, and natural cosmetics business.

CHAPTER 1: The Nirma Washing Powder's Success Story

The success story of the famous Nirma washing powder began in a small Gujarati farmer's house. We'll tell you about a billionaire father who lost his daughter in a car crash and later discovered a way to get her back to life. When she was alive, only a few people knew of her daughter, but it was the sheer persistence and willpower of this man that made his daughter famous in the world, even though she was no more. This is the story of a man who was born into a poor farming family and turned his daughter's nickname into India's leading detergent, soda ash, and education brand. A man of valor and passion who showed that nothing will hinder you if you have the willpower. Here is the story of **"Sabki Pasand Nirma, Washing Powder Nirma."**

1.1 Invention of Nirma detergent?

Karsanbhai was born in Ruppur, Gujarat, to a farmer's family in 1945. He had earned a bachelor's degree in chemistry by the age of 21. He attempted to do a normal job like his colleagues at first. He served as a lab technician for the Lalbhai Group's New Cotton Mills, which is credited with launching the Indian jeans movement. He also took up a position at the Geology and Mining Department of the Gujarat government after this short stint. The year 1969 marked the start of a turning point in the career trajectory of Karsanbhai. It was at this time that Hindustan Lever Ltd (now Hindustan Unilever) formed a full monopoly on the Indian detergent market under the brand name "Surf." A Surf Pack was sold somewhere from Rs 10-15 back then. The USP was that, unlike normal washing soap bars, it eliminated stains from your clothes and didn't irritate your skin. However, for middle-class families, which had no other choice than to return to the old bar soap, this price point was not affordable. The tycoon in Karsanbhai noticed the issue and devised a plan. A young Karsanbhai will come home from work and dedicate all his time and energy to making a phosphate-free detergent in his yard. He wanted to bear in mind that he needed to produce a detergent with a low manufacturing cost so that everybody could afford it. Karsanbhai utilized a recipe for a yellow-colored detergent powder that could be marketed for a mere Rs 3 after several trials and failures. He chose to name the invention after Nirupama, his daughter. He finally got the formula right one day, and as an after-work business, he began making detergents in his 100-square-foot backyard. He will cycle around the neighborhoods, selling door-to-door homemade detergent packages. Patel set the price of his detergent at Rs. 3, almost a third less than Hindustan Unilever's well-known brand "Surf." The product's high quality and low price made it a success, and it was well-received by many who saw great benefit in purchasing it. Because of the business's high promise, Karsanbhai quit his government job three years later to pursue it full-time. Karsanbhai was so fond of the commodity that he called it Nirma, after his daughter Nirupama's nickname. To make sure that everybody remembers her, he used her picture (the girl in the white frock) on the pack and in TV advertisements. Such was a father's love for his daughter. While Karsanbhai Patel himself was not an MBA graduate, the techniques he adopted to expand his company left marketers bewildered and amazed. 'Nirma' was not only a game-changer but also a trendsetter for several small companies. Here are a couple of 'Washing Powder Nirma's' management lessons.

1.2 Karsanbhai Patel's sale policy for Nirma detergent

Karsanbhai Patel agreed to start marketing it once the product had a strong formula. On his cycle, he used to go door-to-door and neighborhood-to-neighborhood every day for three years, pitching the detergent. As it was a brand new product, if they found the product poor, he gave his consumers a money-back guarantee. Nirma has been the cheapest detergent in Ahmedabad at the time. As a result, Karsanbhai's product was an immediate hit. He left his government job three years later and set up a store in Ahmedabad to carry out this full-time enterprise. In some areas of Gujarat, his brand was doing very well, but there was a need to expand its scope. At the time, the standard was to offer the product to retailers on credit. This was a huge gamble because if the product didn't sell, Karsanbhai would have had to close down the company. At that time, he chose to try something different. He planned to spend a little money on advertising. These commercials, with their catchy jingles, were directed at housewives. And this bet paid off well. Nirma became a famous household brand and it had to be purchased by people. He did, however, remove 90% of the stock from the market at this time. Potential buyers had asked for the detergent at their local retailers for about a full month but would have to return empty-handed. During this time, retail store owners flocked to Karsanbhai, demanding that the detergent supply be increased. After another month, he eventually decided. Nirma was able to take over the sales and even beat Surf at their own game due to this approach. It went on to become the country's highest-selling detergent. It remained India's largest-selling detergent even after a decade,

1.3 Invest In Research and Development

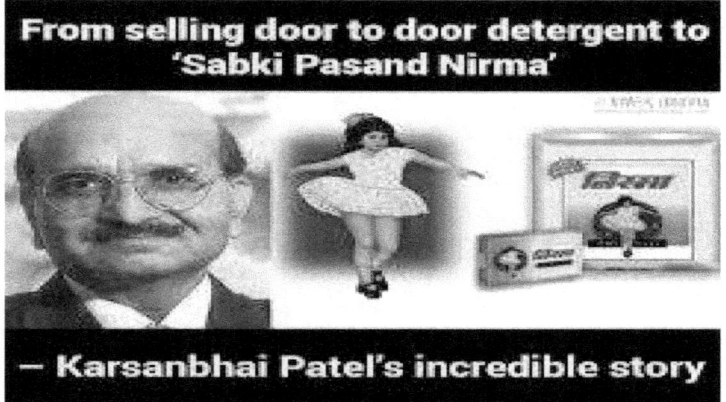

Karsanbhai Patel had little means and was not a man born with a silver spoon in his mouth. Karsanbhai loved experimenting with chemicals after completing a B.Sc. in Chemistry at the age of 21 and then working as a laboratory technician. He noticed that only MNCs in India were selling detergents and there was no economy brand detergent for the country. His excitement about bridging the distance grew, sensing a massive opening, and Karsanbhai began experimenting with chemicals. He quickly succeeded in manufacturing a detergent of high quality at a much cheaper price, which was an immediate success in the industry. Every good product needs a substantial expenditure in time, resources, and commitment in research and development.

1.4 No Higher Costs

Nirma had rewritten the rules of the game within a short time, by delivering high-quality goods at an unprecedentedly low price. Nirma's success was due to its cost-cutting policy. Patel had concentrated from the very beginning on delivering high-value goods at the lowest price possible. The corporation sought to keep improving efficiency while reducing prices. Nirma sought out captive processing plants for raw materials to keep production costs to a minimum. This led to the backward integration initiative, as part of which, at Baroda and Bhavnagar, which became operational in 2000, two state-of-the-art plants were established. This also led to a reduction in raw-material prices. Ahead of time and at a much smaller cost than anticipated, the two new plants were completed. The Baroda plant's second phase was finished 6 months ahead of schedule and at a cost of Rs.2.5 billion compared to the initial projected cost of Rs. 2.8 billion. Compared to the initial projected cost of Rs. 10.36 billion, the Bhavnagar plant was finished in a record period of 2 years at a cost of Rs.9.86 billion. This plant had a workforce of just 500 employees. Concerning Nirma's plant, Tata Chemical's plant, which had around twice the amount, employed ten times the number of workers. Almost

65000 tpa of N-Paraffin was produced by the Baroda plant for Linear Alkyl Benzene (LAB) and Synthetic detergents. Similarly, almost 4.20,000 tpa of soda ash could be produced by the Bhavnagar facility. Akzo Nobel Engineering in Holland produced the Akzo Dry Lime technology used in this factory. The plant had 108 kilometers of salt bunds, which would assist in the potential development of vacuum iodized salt. Patel said, "We have a processing potential of three lakh tons of pure salt. No one in the world had a related plant, but Tata Salt." Nirma had reduced its distribution costs by obviating the need for middlemen. The item went to the dealer straight from the manufacturer. Hiren K Patel (Hiren), CMD, explained to Nirma Customer Care Ltd., "An order is placed and the truck immediately leaves. It's similar to a bank account. We're sending stock, they're sending money." In states like Tamil Nadu, Andhra Pradesh, and southern Karnataka, the company-maintained depots, as it was often difficult to bring stocks to these regions. Stocks were shipped directly from the plants in states like Madhya Pradesh and Uttar Pradesh. In March 2000, Nirma opted for in-house packaging and printing by obtaining Kisan Factories at Moriya, near Ahmedabad, in a further cost-cutting exercise. Nirma hoped that this would increase the packaging's quality.

1.5 Be Proactive in your approach as it is beneficial for the business

Karsanbhai Patel was the only person who started this business and starting selling Nirma. He was educated and had a government career, but he was never afraid of selling door-to-door detergent. He was diligent in doing something and knew that the company was tiny and bootstrapping, so he had to consider everything and anything about his business that could be fruitful. There is no such thing as a small or large undertaking. And if you are the CEO, you should embrace the obligations that are valuable to the company without guilt.

1.6 Provide Customers with 'Value for Money'

Customers noticed the advantages of purchasing Nirma, and it became an immediate success. They considered the standard to be at par with the giant Surf brand, but to take advantage of the same perks, they just had to pay one-third of the amount. Customers would only appreciate the product if you show them the advantages and give them decent value for their money.

1.7 Define Your Segment

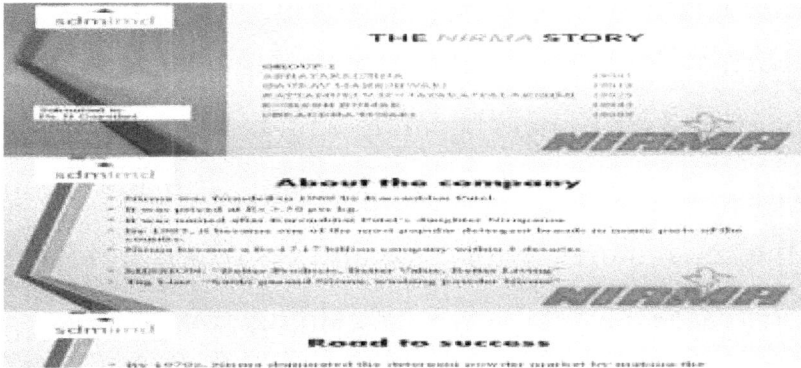

Karsanbhai Patel identified the target segment for his detergent almost as soon as he found the magical formula. He realized that a luxury brand sold in tier 1 cities was the alternative Surf brand, so he concentrated on marketing his brand in tier 2-3 cities. He priced his detergent low and made it a mass brand to get more consumer traction. People from the lower middle class and middle class quickly adopted the product, and it quickly rose in popularity. Where most firms adopted the conventional top-down strategy, i.e., spreading from metro towns to rural cities, Nirma did the reverse and changed the whole game. It is really important to evaluate the competitors for every company and define the most lucrative segment.

1.8 Focus on Building a Brand

It was failing to find vendors outside the city in the early 80s, although the commodity was approved on a small scale in Ahmedabad. Since clients were unaware of its presence, retailers were wary of keeping the detergent in their stores. It resulted in overdue payments, return on inventory, and large business losses. Karsanbhai Patel came up with a good publicity approach to handle the situation and launched a TV advertisement campaign. The popular "Washing powder Nirma, detergent tikiya Nirma" jingle became an anthem for the company and customers began to equate Nirma as a strong brand. The demand for Nirma soon peaked, and with his products, Patel flooded the retail stores. A good brand decreases a buyer's potential risk and increases the company's bargaining power.

1.9 Astutely Manage the Brand Wars

Nirma also had innovative marketing campaigns. Nirma successfully spread the name to other product segments in the mid-nineties, such as premium detergents (Nirma Mega Detergent Cake and Washing Powder), premium toilet soaps, and (Nirma Sandal, Nima Premium, Nirma Lime Fresh). In both the economy and luxury markets, it maintained its initial pricing and marketing plans. In 2000, with Nirma Beauty Shampoo, Nirma Shikakai, and Toothpaste, the firm entered the hair care market. Soaps, unlike detergents, were a private-care commodity. Many consumers had strong emotional attachments with their soap products. Furthermore, HLL segmented the market by price, fragrance appeal, and brand personality. So, against Lifebuoy, Nirma put Nirma Wash, Nirma Beauty Soap against Lux, Nima Rose against Breeze7, and Nirma Lime against Jai Lime. Explaining how Nirma hoped to win this match, playing by the rules of HLL, Hiren said"Worldwide, there are only four or five channels that account for most of the soaps sold: floral, fashion, fitness, freshness." With the relevant scents, Nirma manufactured high-fatty-matter soaps and priced them much lower than other brands. As a result, the 'sub-premium' section was born. The game of controlling the geographical variety of market desires was also perfected by Nirma. The North, for instance, favored pink soaps, and green ones were favored by the South. In the South, sandal soaps were more common. Initially, the company's promotional budget, relative to other FMCG firms, was very poor. In contrast to the usual 6-10 percent, Nirma spent just 1.25-2 percent of its sales on ads. The firm used starlets such as Sangeeta Bijlani, Sonali Bendre, and Riya Sen, who were comparatively unknown at the time, to endorse soaps. The promotional messages were both transparent and centered on the product's benefits. Nirma still chose to first put the item on the shelf, get reviews, and then create a lasting ad campaign. Nirma used its tried-and-true tool, price, to introduce toilet soaps and detergents in the premium market. In these divisions, the company intended to rely on quantities as well. However, the margins granted to retailers had shifted. Unlike economic goods, where the cost advantages were passed on to customers, this advantage was passed on to retailers by Nirma. It provided them with massive profit margins. For instance, it offered 52 percent for Nirma premium soap and an incredible margin of 140 percent for Nirma shampoo. In the luxury segment of the soap industry, observers were pessimistic about Nirma's chances of success.

Unlike detergents, the demand for soaps and shampoos was incredibly fragmented. There were only 15-20 brands, and it was hard to get a considerable market share for any soap. This market was also less price sensitive. So, it was hard for any enterprise to support itself on price alone. Analysts thought that shifting the brand value of Nirma would take years. According to a survey conducted by Nirma's marketing agency, Samsika Marketing Consultancy, Nirma was viewed as a low-cost brand. Many people were almost afraid to say they used it. Nirma published corporate advertisements worth Rs 10 bn in India in the late nineties to shed this image. Analysts claim that the fast-growing shampoo market is a safer investment than luxury soaps. Just 30% of the population in India used shampoo, with more than 70% of this group living in urban areas. However, according to some researchers, while the rural market's presumed potential was very high, it was difficult to convince rural folk to use shampoos in actual practice. A further concern faced by Nirma was that of insufficient facilities. While it had a good presence in the smaller towns and villages, it lacked the requisite network for urban centers to penetrate. As a result, Nirma's foray into high-end soaps and shampoos proved to be a flop.

1.10 Diversify the Portfolio

For low-income groups, Nirma began with a low-cost detergent, but later introduced products for higher-income groups, such as Nirma Sandal soap, Nirma Beauty soap, etc.

Not just that, but in 2003, Karsanbhai Patel formed Nirma University to diversify the company's brand portfolio. The brand is currently exploring its options in the cement industry to grow its market. Diversifying the portfolio decreases the company's potential risk of loss while still allowing it to serve a broader variety of consumers.

1.11 Conclusion

While Nirma was best known as a manufacturer of goods for the low-cost economy, it was popular in the middle and upmarket segments. Yet rivalry was also growing at the same time. Although HLL continued to be a major threat, offensive initiatives were also introduced by P&G and Henkel SPIC. In the detergent and washing powder market, participants from the unorganized field were also introduced to the rivalry. Patel was confident of tackling the rivalry, though. "He added, "We keep the price line and the happy customer returns to us normally. Based on its growth strategy, the company has risen in demand and volume in the last three decades: "A buyer is not looking for one-time frills or feel-good variables. The landlord, on the other hand, is searching for a long-term solution to his or her issues." Karsanbhai Patel, who began with a vision of making his daughter famous through his brand and ended up being one of the greatest entrepreneurs of all time, exemplifies the relevance of this quotation. He began with an aim of creating his daughter famous through his brand and ended up becoming one of the greatest entrepreneurs of all time. His name not only gained tremendous respect but also became a trendsetter for many new firms. The brand has taught young entrepreneurs many useful lessons and has proven to be a valuable resource for the region. Karsanbhai Patel has shown that no goal is too lofty if you have the ambition and zeal to achieve it.

1.12 What Karsanbhai Patel and Nirma detergent did for the Indian Economy

Nirma's meteoric growth in prominence culminated in the introduction of a new economic market for detergent powder. It was of good quality and was inexpensive. Plus, contrary to the others, the fact that it was manufactured without phosphates made it the most environmentally-friendly detergent. In comparison, a labor-consuming process was the process of producing the detergent. And thus, Nirma went on to hire more than 14,000 workers and became the country's leading employer.

1.13 Karsanbhai Patel's ventures other than the Nirma detergent

Karsanbhai wanted to grow his FMCG business after Nirma dominated the detergent industry. Nirma launched its line of toilet soaps, beauty soaps, and even shampoos in the premium market.

While the latter venture failed, one of their products, edible salt Shudh, is still available and doing well. Overall, Nirma has a 20 percent market share in soap cakes and a 35 percent market share in detergents. That isn't it, however. In 1995, Karsanbhai Patel founded the Nirma Institute of Technology in Ahmedabad. Later, it became one of Gujarat's most prestigious engineering schools. After that, the whole structure was merged under the Nirma University of Science and Technology, which is supervised by the Nirma Education and Research Foundation, and in 2003, the entire structure was unified under the Nirma University of Science and Technology. This is overseen by the Nirma Education and Research Foundation. Since 2004, Karsanbhai's CSR initiative, Nirmalabs education, has aimed to train and incubate entrepreneurs. Karsanbhai Patel has now turned over the reins of his profitable company to his two sons. Pratibha Patil, the then-President of India, bestowed the Padma Shri on him in 2010. Nirma is now the world's biggest manufacturer of soda ash, and the company has been privately owned since 2012. Karsanbhai Patel invested his huge fortune on a six-seat chopper in 2013, which cost Rs 40 crore. After Gautam Adani (Adani Group) and Pankaj Patel (Zydus Group), he became the third Ahmedabad-based industrialist to purchase a helicopter. Nirma, on the other hand, is still one of India's most popular detergents. And the jingles will live on forever.

CHAPTER 2: Start a Profitable Soap Making Business

As a soap manufacturer, you'll create your recipes for soaps and probably other personal cleaning and beauty products. Ecommerce, farmers markets, arts events, wholesale positioning in spas and boutiques, and even door-to-door sales are all options for selling the goods. You'll test several solutions and see if you can find a steady stream of clients. Learn how to launch a soap-making company of your own.

Steps for starting a soap making business

You've uncovered the ideal market opportunity and are now prepared to take the next step. There's more to launching a company than simply filing papers with the government. We've put together a list of steps to help you get started with your soap-making business. These measures will ensure that the new company is well-planned, legally compliant, and properly registered.

Plan your business

As an entrepreneur, you must have a well-thought-out strategy. It will assist you in figuring out the additional data of your organization and uncovering any unknowns. Given below are some key points to consider:

What are the startup and recurring costs?

Who is the targeted audience?

What is the maximum price you will charge from the customers?

What would you name your company?

What are the costs involved in opening a soap-making business?

You've got a good start if you have a kitchen or workspace as well as a few simple kitchen utensils. Making soap isn't an expensive business to undertake, but you would need to invest in some basic equipment. Ingredients cost at least $200. Lye and fats or oils are used to make soap. That's a good start, but it'll be your special formula that sets you apart. For superior feel, fragrance, and lather, you can use coconut oil, olive oil, almond oil, and several fragrance oils, extracts, and natural additives. To keep materials costs down and simplify production, you could start with only one or two simple recipes. Equipment for producing soap will cost around $300. Your equipment specifications will be determined by the type of soap-making you do. Hot process, cold process, rebatching, and melt and pour are the four basic forms of processing, and each needs different equipment. But, regardless of the route you take, you'll almost definitely need soap molds, packing, and shipping items. You can get your basic ingredients, additives, equipment, and supplies from several online retailers. Marketing software will cost up to $750. A professional-looking website with enticing product images is key to the company's growth. Since your online consumers can't touch or smell your goods, they must be able to judge the good quality of what they see. That means recruiting a graphic designer and web developer to help you make the best out of your logo and online presence is a smart investment. To express your love and dedication to product quality, your visual imagery will be carried through in your labeling and branding. Skilled services will cost up to $200. Is it legal in your state and society for you to run this sort of business from home? Before you put up your shingle, meet with a lawyer for a quick consultation. The Handcrafted Soap & Cosmetics Guild charges a membership fee of $100 per year (HSCG). Small-batch soap makers will benefit from this organization's preparation, funding, and useful networking opportunities. Insurance for general liability and product liability would cost $265-$375 a year. This is also accessible via the HSCG.

What are the ongoing expenses for a soap-making business?

The consumable commodity materials you'll need for ongoing development would be your greatest ongoing expense. Your increasing variable expenses would be more than offset by a rise in revenue if you've priced your offering correctly.

Who is the target market?

While women make up the majority of the demand for homemade soaps, some firms have had success selling male-oriented soap scents. You may approach consumers who admire your product's consistency and luxury, or those who only purchase organic or vegan goods. Customers will note the difference in quality among your soaps and those sold on the shelves of a traditional supermarket.

How does a soap-making business make money?

In the majority of the cases, all of your revenue shall be derived from the products you make or sell.

How much can you charge customers?

Your goods could be sold for $5 or $6 a bar. This is more than your consumers are likely to spend for mass-produced retail soaps, but your product has a high perceived value. Other price points can be met by providing discounts on multiple orders, marketing multi-bar bundles, and extending the product range. Look at local rivals' websites to see what they're costing and how that would impact the pricing. Will you charge more to suggest a higher-end product range, or will you charge less to compensate for the lower per-unit sales margin with higher volume?

How much profit can a soap-making business make?

There are a few well-known soap makers who began their careers in the same way you did. Take, for example, Burt's Bees. Others in your business run it as a side venture, something between a crafts hobby and a modestly profitable business. You will go as far as your dedication, imagination, promotional skills, and hard work can take you, as with many home-based companies.

How can you make your business more profitable?

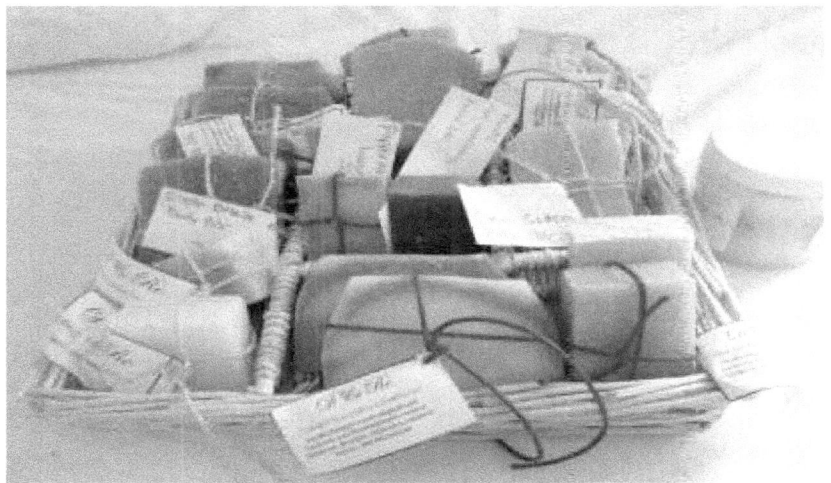

Many soap makers diversify their product range to include more exotic soaps (goat's milk soap is one example) or complementary goods. Making candles is a natural progression for soap makers who still use a hot process. Others are involved in home fragrances, lip balms, hair care, and even pet products. Focus on what else will cater to the consumer base when speaking about expanding your product mix. Many companies aim to maximize their net income by lowering the cost of goods produced. Growing the earnings by issuing bigger batches at a time is a cost-effective technique.

2.1 What will you name your business?

Choosing the correct name is vital and daunting. If you own a sole proprietorship, you should start using a separate company name from your own. We suggest reviewing the following references before filing a company name:

The state's business records

Federal and state trademark records

Social media sites

Web domain availability

It's important to have your domain name registered before anyone else does.

2.2 Form a legal entity

The sole proprietorship, partnership, limited liability company (LLC), and corporation are the most traditional corporate structures. If your soap manufacturing company is used, creating a legitimate business entity such as an LLC or corporation prevents you from being found legally accountable.

Register for taxes

Before you can start doing business, you'll need to apply for several state and federal taxes. You would need to apply for an EIN to pay for taxation. It's very basic and free.

2.3 Small Business Taxes

Depending on which business arrangement you select, you can have various taxation choices for your corporation. There could be state-specific taxes that apply to your business. In the state sales tax guides, you can read more about state sales taxes and franchise taxes.

2.4 Open a business bank account & credit card

Personal wealth security necessitates the use of dedicated company banking and credit accounts. If your personal and corporate accounts are combined, your personal properties (such as your house, vehicle, and other valuables) are put at risk if your company-issued. This is referred to as piercing the corporate veil in business law. Furthermore, learning how to create company credit will help you receive credit cards and other borrowings under your business's name (rather than your own), lower interest rates, and more credit lines, among other advantages.

2.5 Open a business bank account

This protects your assets from those of your business, which is essential for personal wealth security, as well as making accounting and tax reporting simpler.

2.6 Get a business credit card

It will help you achieve the following benefits:

It builds the company's credit background and will be beneficial for raising capital and profit later on.

It lets you differentiate personal and business expenditures by placing all of your business's costs under one account.

Set up business accounting

Understanding your business's financial results includes keeping track of your different costs and sources of revenue. Maintaining correct and comprehensive reports also makes annual tax filing even simpler.

2.7 Obtain necessary permits and licenses

Failure to obtain required permits and licenses will result in hefty fines or even the closure of your company. If you intend to market homemade soaps, you must first acquire a business license.

2.8 State & Local Business Licensing Requirements

Operating a handmade soap company can necessitate the procurement of some state permits and licenses. Furthermore, several states have varying laws governing the manufacturing of cosmetics and other body care goods. Visit the SBA's guide to state licenses and permits to read more about your state's licensing criteria.

2.9 Labor safety requirements

It is essential to comply with all Occupational Safety and Health Administration protocols. Pertinent requirements include:

Employee injury report

Safety signage

2.10 Certificate of Occupancy

A Certificate of Occupancy is normally required for businesses that operate out of a specific location (CO). All requirements concerning building codes, zoning rules, and local requirements have been followed, according to a CO. If you're thinking about renting a space, keep the following in mind:

Securing a CO is normally the landlord's duty.

Before signing a contract, make sure your landlord has or can get a legitimate CO for a soap-making operation.

A new CO is often needed after a significant renovation. If your company will be renovated before opening, add wording in your lease agreement that specifies that lease payments will not begin before a valid CO is issued.

If you intend to buy or build a place:

You would be responsible for securing a legal CO from a local government body.

Review all building codes and zoning standards for your soap-making business's place to ensure that you'll comply and eligible to get a CO.

2.11 Trademark & Copyright Protection

It is wise to protect your interests by applying for the required trademarks and copyrights if you are creating a new product, idea, brand, or design. The essence of legal standards in distance education is continually evolving, especially when it comes to copyright laws. This is a regularly revised database that can assist you with keeping on top of legal specifications.

2.12 Get business insurance

Insurance, including licenses and permits, are necessary for your company to run safely and legally. In the case of a covered loss, corporate insurance covers your company's financial well-being. There are several insurance schemes tailored for diverse types of companies with various risks. If you're not sure what kinds of risks your company might face, start with General Liability Insurance. This is the most popular form of coverage required by small companies, so it's a good place to start.

2.13 Learn more about General Liability Insurance

Workers' Compensation Insurance is another essential insurance scheme that many companies need. When your company hires staff, your state may mandate you to carry the Workers' Benefits Package.

2.14 Define your brand

Your company's brand is what it stands for, as well as how the general public perceives it. A good name would set the company apart from the market.

How to promote & market a soap making business

Look for areas where you can stand out. Try having a larger-than-usual bar of soap or one that is formulated to last longer. Perhaps you should market a six-pack of sampler soaps in smaller sizes so that your customers can check out your whole product range and pick their preferences. Consider an uncommon fragrance or texture additive for applying to your soaps to make them stand out. When you've found a winning design, publicize it on your website and social media. Also, if you're showing your soaps at an exhibition, bring some unwrapped samples of your entire product line so consumers can touch them, see what they're made of, feel their textures, and experience the various scents.

How to keep customers coming back

bear in mind that you're offering an aesthetic experience. Make sure your logo, labels and packages, and the name of your product line all cater to consumers looking for a low-cost luxury experience. One benefit is that the more your consumers like your stuff, the faster they can consume it and require more. Ensure that you retain contact with your clients and that they are aware of how to contact you. Request email addresses from all of your clients to obtain their approval to send out a monthly e-newsletter or catalog. It's important not to bother someone with so many promotional newsletters, but a monthly newsletter will keep consumers updated on all of the new items you have to sell. You might want to add a toll-free phone number for orders as your company expands.

Establish your web presence

Customers can learn more about your business and the goods or services you deliver by visiting your website. One of the most successful ways to build your web presence is through press releases and social media.

2.15 Soap Making Plan

If you live in the jungle and love your body odor, you would not need soap. It is a regular need and one of the common goods. As a result, soap has a huge demand. There are various varieties of soaps available due to the wide range of skin types. Soaps are manufactured in a multitude of ways to suit the needs of all. One of the most promising FMCGs is soap production. Perhaps this is why so many people are drawn to this sector year after year. Every day, in a country like India, there is a massive demand for soap. However, there are only a few competitors in the business. We have a few ideas for you if you want to launch your own soap company. Let's get this started.

Tips for soap making using the cold process method

Soap making is easy at the most fundamental level. The cold process approach is the most common way to produce soap. It's "cold" because the ingredients aren't heated before being combined. Using the "hot process" technique, you can make soap with heat. We will use the cold process. Soap is made by mixing fats and oils with a lye and water solution in the most basic form. Soap is made from a combination of water, lye, fats, and oils. The fun starts as you change the components and quantities of the various materials. But, to keep things simple, note that soap is essentially a solution of fats and oils, lye, and water. It's as plain as that.

Is making soap without lye possible?

Is it possible to produce soap without lye? Not at all. Soap bases that can be heated and poured into molds can be purchased. You didn't have to use lye to make the base as everyone else did. However, you have no idea what's in those bases. Sodium hydroxide is the lye used to produce bar soap. Soft soaps are made of potassium hydroxide. Leaching lye from wood ashes is an easy way to create it. This form of lye results in a smoother soap. Unless you have access to a chemical supply house, lye is typically difficult to come by locally. It is, however, simple to put an order. Lye is highly caustic, and it can sear the skin and strip color from whatever surface it comes into contact with. If it gets into your eyes, it will blind you. This is a toxic drug and can never be used in a place where children may reach it. Adults, on the other hand, would have no trouble with the lye if they take simple precautions. When dealing with lye, please wear safety goggles. Long sleeves and protective gloves are also recommended. Leave lye or lye mixtures unattended at all times. Uncured soap should be used similarly to lye.

Fats and oils required for making the cold process soap

Another fundamental to producing soap can be found here. To turn oils and fats into soap, different quantities of lye are needed. Every fat that is likely to be used in soap making has a known amount of time it takes to turn oil or fat into soap. Simply look up the amount of lye needed to produce soap from a certain oil in a table. The volume of lye used in each recipe is then determined based on the oils used. Using a little less lye than is needed to transform all of the oils into soap. This is achieved as a precautionary step to ensure that all of the lye is absorbed during the process. The lye discount is the volume of lye used that is reduced. It's normal to use around 5% less lye than is needed to completely transform the oils into soap. Coconut, palm, and olive oils are the most common oils used in soap making. If you just use those three oils to make soap, you will make amazing results. Each of these oils has its collection of characteristics that make it useful as a soaping oil. You can produce a soap with only one of the oils, but the results won't be as strong as if you used all three. This is why. If you want a lot of bubbles in your soap, coconut oil is the way to go. It's the root of a slew of big, light bubbles. However, soap made entirely of coconut oil cleans so well that it extracts much of the oil from the skin, leaving it dry. This is why it can only account for about 30% of the soap oils. Palm oil is important for hard, long-lasting bars, but it isn't as clean or bubbly as coconut oil. This fat is often referred to as "vegetable tallow," but it is similar to beef tallow in any way. If you don't want to eat meat fats, use them instead of beef fat. Then you should ask about olive oil. Just olive oil is used to produce castile soap conventionally. If you've ever used this form of soap, you know how good it is as a skin conditioner. It's amazing. However, if olive oil is the only oil used in the soap, the effect is tiny little bubbles and bars that fade away quicker than you'd like. As a result, this type of oil is only used to make up about 40% of the oils in a recipe. Granted, soap can be made from almost any form of fat or oil, and there are several alternatives.

Adding ingredients for premium luxury results

If you choose to use other oils, just apply a small amount during the final stages of the soap-making process. you'll find that you can use almond oil in your example recipe. Simply raise the amount of olive oil in the formula and leave out the almond oil. It was chosen because it brings a little more to the bar's feel and quality. Soap can be used for a lot more than just producing pure soap. All of the additives are what make soap production so exciting. Clays, natural oils, medicinal products, colors, patterns, and a slew of other alternatives are available as additives. The first step to perfect soap is to get the fundamentals correctly, which can be achieved fast and effectively. After learning the fundamentals of soap manufacturing, the soap manufacturer progresses to using a range of exotic ingredients.

How to make soap?

We'll go into the fundamentals of how the soap is made. Bear in mind that this is just the first step. Following that, you may need additional materials and a special recipe to distinguish the product from competitors.

Ingredients

Given below are the following ingredients that would be required for preparing soap:

Take 2/3 cup of coconut oil (that will create lather) and the same amount of olive oil. Moreover, 2/3 cup almond, safflower oil, or grape seed will also be needed.

Then you'll need a quarter cup of lye, which is sodium hydroxide in its purest form. Finally, you'll require 3/4 cup of cool water that is distilled or pure.

You'll also need oatmeal, aloe vera gel, cornmeal, clay, salt, and any other items you choose to use.

Instructions

Listed below are the step-by-step directions that you must follow in the preparation of soap:

Put on your gloves and pour lye and water into a canning jar. Allow them to sit for a few minutes after they've been stirred gently and the water has begun to clear.

Now pour in the oil from the pint jar. Then Stir well, then put the jar in a warm pan of the water that is bubbling (and/or you may microwave it, when you do, place temperature to one hundred and twenty degrees F).

Remove the lye after that is finished. Allow the lye to cool. Remove pint jar & allow your oil to cool as well. Both can achieve a temperature of 95 to 105 degrees Fahrenheit. If the temperature drops below 95 degrees F, the soap will begin to crumble.

Pour them into a mixing bowl until they've hit the ideal temperature and whisk until fully combined. After stirring for five minutes, mix it with an immersion blender.

Then, to make the soap special, apply herbs, essential oils, & any other things that go with it. They can be thoroughly combined so they appear coarse. Place them in molds & cover with a towel.

After a day check the soap and let it stay for an additional 12 to 24 hours if it's either warm or soft.

When the soaps are fully cured, wrap them in the paper wax & lock them in an airtight jar for a week. Since this soap contains oil on its own, we'll need an airtight jar. As a consequence, interaction with air will cause it to pick up debris and dust.

Soap making machine and price

fiber covered mixing machine will cost you at least about US$ 1000. This price includes a fiber-covered mixing machine capable of producing 200 kilograms of detergent powder.

Where to get soap making machine?

Online, you can buy a soap-manufacturing machine. Soap manufacturing machines are available from several online retailers.

These websites sell the requisite appliances, including the microwave, blender, wrapper, mold, and labeler, also the main device. A soap-making unit, for example, can be bought for the US $ 5000. This item can be used to produce toilet soaps and detergent cakes. If you're searching for something less costly, say under the US $ 1500 apiece, you can easily find it on the market. It can be used to produce soap for bathing purposes. There are also other products of varying price points. However, the budget may start at one dollar an item. You'll get a good detergent maker for this amount.

Soap making raw material and price

The Soap-making ingredients may be bought for a very cheap price. It is much less costly if you buy them in bulk. If you may get the price correct upfront, the rest of the company will be a breeze later on. As a consequence, we prefer bulk raw materials. Alkali and fat are the two main raw materials used to produce soap. the raw material which is most commonly used in soap manufacture is sodium hydroxide. Potassium hydroxide, on the other hand, maybe used. The latter makes a soap that is more soluble in water. As a result, potassium hydroxide creates "warm soap." Locally, raw products are available at a reduced quality. You can discover raw materials for manufacturing soaps online or in your neighborhood with a fast Google search. People typically buy this locally so it cuts the price even further. Rest assured that rates can differ depending on your needs. It depends solely on how much you're making & how much of the raw material you'll need. Caustic soda costs about US $ 150-250 per metric ton on the market. The price of 1000 grams of laundry soap ranges between US$1 and $1.25.

Soap making formulae

legitimate chemical formulae for the soap's $C_{17}H_{35}COONa$. Its chemical name is thus sodium stearate. However, it is important to note that it's for the common soap that is used for personal purposes only. For the detergents, there are normally long chains of carboxylic acid as well as sulfonate salts or ammonium salt.

2.16 Soap selling process

Let us now go through the packaging, distribution, marketing, and promotion processes.

Colorful wrappings

Choose a bright & eye-catching label that will guarantee that the product is noticed. To set it apart from the competition, style it & use the proper design.

Branding

Make the most of this opportunity to build your brand through packaging. Choose a design that you think best reflects your business.

Go simple

Today's entrepreneurs aim for simplicity. Examine the performance of POP displays as well. If they don't live up to your standards, it's time to make a change.

Soap marketing strategy

You can use the following strategies for marketing soap:

Email marketing

And the ones who also sign up for your offer are truly interested in the soaps, email marketing is the perfect way to market. It's also becoming highly customizable and cost-efficient these days.

Blogging

The next logical move is to start blogging. You'll need to hunt down some prominent bloggers who may help you spread the word about the business. You may even invite them to write a review on their blog about a sample of the product.

Social media

Due to availability of the social media, it is now easier to create a brand. Furthermore, guess what? It's the shortest and least expensive alternative. The secret is to make something go viral. this could be the merchandise, online presence, or your ads.

2.17 Soap making supplies

To make it function properly, you'll need some modernized tools equipment, as well as a lot of the space. You will need to find rental space to make the soap. Some of the typical things you'll need to get started include cyclone, mixing vessels, perfumers, blowers, reactors, furnaces, weighing scales, and blenders.

2.18 Marketing area for soap

The marketing region you select will be decided by the audience you're targeting. You would be able to segment your customers depending on age and demographic in social media marketing. Your marketing field can be decided by the type of soap you sell. If you're selling detergent cakes, for example, they're mainly aimed at homemakers of different ages. As a consequence, you will show the commercial depending on age & gender. Marketing is successful on a variety of measures. It simply depends upon whether you've online or a physical company. In any case, it's better to entrust this to a practitioner.

2.19 Total investment

The Investment isn't based on raw materials. Just As mentioned above, different raw materials are used for personal and detergent soaps. Therefore investment will be different for each category.

You must take into consideration the size and place of the business for starting the business. So You need minimum money of US $ 20,000to purchase the machinery along with primary raw materials –if you decide to start with little.

Raw materials shall cost the US $ 2500 per month. Moreover, making unit rentals would charge not less than the US $ 1000 per month. In addition to the above-mentioned costs, the salary of the plant manager is expected to be around the US $ 500. Equipment shall cost around the US $ 10,000 or more.

In addition to the above prices, you need the US $ 500 for license & registration. Moreover, you will need another US $ 800 to cover the accidental coverage. the Marketing might cost you approximately US $ 500 per month.

2.20 Selling price

Supply, materials, brand, packaging, and other factors impact soap pricing. When you're only starting, keep the rates comparable to those of your rivals.

Prices are determined by several factors. A lower-cost soap is generally assumed to be of lower quality. As a result, we won't keep prices very low about market prices.

Additionally, too high prices could decrease overall demand. As a consequence, we will arrive at the golden middle & retain it just marginally, so at all, below current levels.

2.21 Profit margin

Measure profit margins through factoring in your annual manufacturing expenses. You must also remember manpower, raw materials, utilities, and maintenance costs.

This business has a high-profit margin, but it also has a lot of competition from well-known brands. As a result, profit margins would be dictated by the price of the goods.

Know more about your rivals' prices and, as a result, determine which would give the greatest return – find the "golden value point" for the sales.

2.22 Precaution

It is important to obtain insurance. it is why, in addition to other necessities, insurance must still be part of the investment.

Another crucial step's to understand the company's legal framework. Obtain both the "consent to establish" and "consent to operate."

2.23 Risk

In the soap industry, the risk is not creating a large enough brand to compete with the rivals. There are a lot of competitors in the business, so making a name for your company can be challenging.

Another danger is that the company will collapse due to a lack of consumer awareness. To run a good soap company, you must first select the right market.

2.24 Conclusion

Soap production, as satisfying as this is, necessitates thorough study and measured risk-taking. Seeking your niche and launching a company are just simple activities. However, careful preparation and intervention are necessary to make this a success. Make sure you don't undersell yourself & that you also stand out.

2.25 Advantage of starting a soap making business at home

Soap making requires little investment to start with

The supplies needed to make soap can be easily acquired

Equipment required can also be easily acquired

It is comparatively much easier to learn the making of soap

There is already good demand for handmade soap and people are willing to purchase handmade soap,

You can easily specialize in your particular field

It's rather easier to make soap that is both distinctive and different from the existing ones

You can create other products that can gel in with your existing products

You can generate handsome profits by selling soap

It is very easy to locate a market for the soaps

2.26 How Much Money Can You Make Making Soap?

That's a tough question to answer because so much depends on you. And, just to be clear, producing soap is not lucrative. Of course, the

money is in the soap sales. To make money selling a product, much as with any other business endeavor takes a lot of time and commitment.

CHAPTER 3: Start a Profitable Candle Making Business

Candlemakers are extremely professional artisans who pay particular attention to the sensory aesthetics of their products and experienced business people who know how to entice consumers with innovative marketing tactics. Learn how to launch a candle-making company of your own.

3.1 Steps for starting a candle making business

You've uncovered the ideal market opportunity and are now prepared to take the next step. There's more to launching a company than simply filing papers with the government. We've put together a list of steps to help you get started with your candle-making business. These measures will ensure that the new company is well-planned, legally compliant, and properly registered.

Plan your business

As an entrepreneur, you must have a well-thought-out strategy. It will assist you in figuring out the additional data of your organization and uncovering any unknowns. Given below are some key points to consider:

What are the startup and recurring costs?

Who is the targeted audience?

What is the maximum price you will charge from the customers?

What would you name your company?

What are the costs involved in opening a candle-making business?

You will be able to start your business at home, based on local zoning rules, making use of your kitchen heat source as well as utensils. Many online retailers, including Candle Science and CandleChem, offer a starter kit of items. To start, your candle materials shouldn't cost more than a few hundred dollars. This includes:

Paraffin, gel, soy, beeswax, or other wax

Wicks

Jars, tins, or other containers (though bear in mind that if you're just selling pillar candles, you won't need containers)

Fragrance oils

Coloring agents

Packaging materials

Transportation costs of raw goods in and finished products out

Web growth, which can cost anywhere from nothing to a few hundred dollars based on the expertise in the industry and at least properly contributes to some other start-up costs. A booth will cost $100 per day if you intend to showcase your goods at different exhibits and festivals, plus you'll have to pay for fuel and other travel expenses. You can also contact an insurance provider first. Since there is a chance of a fire accident, you can ensure that your company is fire-proofed and that you have a fire extinguisher onboard. You can also have an initial consultation with a lawyer to decide what licenses or permits are required in your region.

What are the ongoing expenses for a candle-making business?

The majority of the business revolves around different varieties of wax, your containers, and paint and scent additives. You can purchase these goods in bulk at lower per-unit prices once you've established your business model is viable. Wax, for example, can be ordered in 25-pound sizes for as little as a dollar per pound. Wicks are sold in 100-foot spools. Bulk amounts of containers, such as glass pots, mason jars, and tins, are also available.

Who is the target market?

Anyone who needs candles is your end customer. Some may have specific concerns, such as lights in the case of a power outage, and others are searching for a more sensory experience. Churches that use candles to decorate prayer offerings or stores that wish to bring a dramatic effect to their showrooms are often fantastic consumers. You may also approach resellers that can order the goods in vast quantities. Shop owners from the neighborhood and beyond will be among them. Customers like these are usually seen at arts and crafts shows. Try renting stalls at arts and crafts shows, flea markets, festivals and fairs, and other similar venues if you love seeing your customers face to face in an atmosphere where they can truly appreciate the aesthetics of your goods.

How does a candle-making business make money?

Candlemakers market candles to customers directly or indirectly through resellers such as boutiques, gift stores, and other arts and crafts shopping outlets. Since candle making is such a wide field, differentiate yourself by the types of candles you sell (pillar, floating, votive, tea, etc.) or the quality of your offering. Experiment with scents, textures, and molds to come up with something unique that is worth premium pricing. Furthermore, for optimum profit margins on your sales, you can still be on the lookout for low-cost raw material suppliers. To widen your target audience, think of related products or candle styles.

3.2 How much can you charge customers?

Your goods could sell for as little as a few bucks or as much as $20 or more per unit. Pricing will be dictated by the nature and reach of your product line, as well as your target market, marketing plan, and competitiveness. If you want to be the lowest vendor, make sure you're buying your raw materials at a discount and that you're still aware of what your rivals are charging. To save the most cost per unit, you'll want to buy wax, wicks, coloring agents, scents, and other products in bulk. If your goal is to market a higher-end product line, price is less important as long as your goods are visually pleasing. If you find a retail reseller that can move a lot of your product, you might want to consider giving deep discounts on prices.

How much profit can a candle-making business make?

Profit margins of 50% or more are not out of the question. While the cost of materials is not especially high, make sure you have the resources to devote to making your company profitable.

How can you make your business more profitable?

Consider expanding the product offerings once you've perfected the principles of candle-making. For example, learning how to mold or carve candles into any shape will improve the cost and revenue potential. Alternatively, you might start selling fancy oil lamps made from liquid candles. Find scented soaps and incense as well as other sensory items. You might be able to learn how to make these additions to your expanding product line, or you might be able to figure out where to purchase them for resale. Consider offering candle-making lessons if you have the requisite space in your workshop. You might contact the local community center or community college in this effort and see if they'd be involved in adding your class to their program. Finally, is the company prosperous enough that you might consider franchising it? You have to give this important factor a thorough consideration if you want to enhance your profits.

What will you name your business?

Choosing the correct name is vital and daunting. If you own a sole proprietorship, you should start using a separate company name from your own. We suggest reviewing the following references before filing a company name:

The state's business records

Federal and state trademark records

Social media sites

Web domain availability

It's important to get your domain name registered before anyone else. After registering a domain name, you should consider setting up a professional email account (@yourcompany.com).

Form a legal entity

The sole proprietorship, partnership, limited liability company (LLC), and corporation are the most traditional corporate structures. If your candle manufacturing company is used, creating a legitimate business entity such as an LLC or corporation prevents you from being found legally accountable.

Register for taxes

Before you can start doing business, you'll need to apply for several state and federal taxes. You would need to apply for an EIN to pay for taxation. It's very basic and free.

Small Business Taxes

Depending on which business arrangement you select, you can have various taxation choices for your corporation. There could be state-specific taxes that apply to your business. In the state sales tax guides, you can read more about state sales taxes and franchise taxes.

Open a business bank account & credit card

Personal wealth security necessitates the use of dedicated company banking and credit accounts. If your personal and corporate accounts are combined, your personal properties (such as your house, vehicle, and other valuables) are put at risk if your company-issued. This is referred to as piercing the corporate veil in business law. Furthermore, learning how to create company credit will help you receive credit cards and another borrowing under your business's name (rather than your own), lower interest rates, and more credit lines, among other advantages.

Open a business bank account

This protects your assets from those of your business, which is essential for personal wealth security, as well as making accounting and tax reporting simpler.

Get a business credit card

It will help you achieve the following benefits:

It builds the company's credit background and will be beneficial for raising capital and profit later on.

It lets you differentiate personal and business expenditures by placing all of your business's costs under one account.

Set up business accounting

Understanding your business's financial results includes keeping track of your different costs and sources of revenue. Maintaining correct and comprehensive reports also makes annual tax filing even simpler.

Labor safety requirements

It is essential to comply with all Occupational Safety and Health Administration protocols. Pertinent requirements include:

Employee injury report

Safety signage

Certificate of Occupancy

A Certificate of Occupancy is normally required for businesses that operate out of a specific location (CO). All requirements concerning building codes, zoning rules, and local requirements have been followed, according to a CO. If you're thinking about renting a space, keep the following in mind:

Securing a CO is normally the landlord's duty.

Before signing a contract, make sure your landlord has or can get a legitimate CO for a soap-making operation.

A new CO is often needed after a significant renovation. If your company will be renovated before opening, add wording in your lease agreement that specifies that lease payments will not begin before a valid CO is issued.

If you intend to buy or build a place:

You would be responsible for securing a legal CO from a local government body.

Review all building codes and zoning standards for your candle-making business's place to ensure that you'll comply and eligible to get a CO.

Trademark & Copyright Protection

It is wise to protect your interests by applying for the required trademarks and copyrights if you are creating a new product, idea, brand, or design. The essence of legal standards in distance education is continually evolving, especially when it comes to copyright laws. This is a regularly revised database that can assist you with keeping on top of legal specifications.

Get business insurance

Insurance, including licenses and permits, are necessary for your company to run safely and legally. In the case of a covered loss, corporate insurance covers your company's financial well-being. There are several insurance schemes tailored for diverse types of companies with various risks. If you're not sure what kinds of risks your company might face, start with General Liability Insurance. This is the most popular form of coverage required by small companies, so it's a good place to start.

Define your brand

Your company's brand is what it stands for, as well as how the general public perceives it. A good name would set the company apart from the market.

How to promote & market a candle making business

The first and most crucial step is to decide who you intend to reach. Is your average customer a cost-conscious shopper, or is she more concerned with the sensory experience? If your target market is the former, you should be able to deliver fair prices. If it's the latter, make sure your product range is well-presented and that your color and scent options are pleasing. Try building an online presence on sites including eBay, Amazon, and Etsy. Since these platforms have a lot of competition, keep the costs as low as possible. There is a slew of other arts and crafts marketplaces, but they aren't as well-known as Etsy (and therefore potentially less populated with competitors). Among them are ArtFire, Big Cartel, and Craft Is Art, to name a few.

How to keep customers coming back

You aim to not only retain buyers but to keep them coming back. Since candles are consumable goods that must be replaced daily, the current consumer partnerships may become profitable over time. As a result, make sure you fulfill their needs so that they appreciate the quality of your goods and know-how to reach you if stocks run out. As a consequence, any order must provide easy-to-find contact information, such as your website, email address, or phone number (or all three). As part of the packaging, you could add a business card or sticker with this detail. Make sure shoppers and passers-by alike get your business card when approaching clients in people, such as at art shows or flea markets. Often, get their names and permission to connect them to an email list you give out, maybe before peak candle-buying seasons like the holidays or Mother's Day.

Establish your web presence

Customers can learn more about your business and the goods or services you deliver by visiting your website. One of the most successful ways to build your online presence is through press releases and social media.

Top of Form

Bottom of Form

Is this Business Right For You?

The perfect candle maker is passionate about the craft and has experience in sales and promotion. Candlemakers may start small, with a minimal budget and inventory, in the kitchen and storage room of their home or apartment. Since candles are always thought of as commodity products, you must continually search for ways to brand your line to set yourself apart from the competition. Excellent image photography, a solid web presence, and savvy sales expertise can help you highlight your product line attractively.

What are some skills and experiences that will help you build a successful candle-making business?

The bulk of people get into this business as hobby candle builders. You should appreciate the aesthetics of making candles and related products and have a clear understanding of how to mark your business. You should be familiar with the principles of eCommerce and how to build an online presence. If you sell from a booth at a fair, your display presentation skills are relevant both online (in the quality of your images and written product descriptions) and in physical displays. If you plan to market your product line in person, either to consumers personally or to resellers, personal sales skill is important. You must trust in the goods and be able to convince people to do so as well.

What is the growth potential for a candle-making business?

A good full-time candle maker could earn between $25,000 and $50,000 per year. However, if you sell to a big reseller, you might make more money. Consider franchising your organization once it has become popular enough for others to choose to follow in your footsteps. Candle making is an easy business to launch on your own. However, your ambition likely is to become so well-known that you'll need assistance with crafting, selling, and/or shipping your merchandise. Begin by enlisting the support of friends or family members if required, such as to match seasonal revenue spikes. Don't recruit permanent full-time support once you've been through ample revenue periods to realize that you'll be able to easily reach payroll over the year. Also, contact the accountant to hear about all the hidden expenses.

Candles Pricing

From a business standpoint, you'll need to find out how much you need/want to receive every hour and how many candles you can make in that time. Divide the hourly wage by the number of units (candles) generated to get a figure to add to the basic cost of the supplies used to manufacture each candle until you have these two numbers. Consider the following scenario: You pay $50 on ingredients (not equipment) and can make 20 candles from them. For the supplies, you paid $2.50 per candle. Making candles is a way for you to earn $20 per hour. Since the 20 candles you made took two hours to make, the overall cost is two times $20, or $40. Then you divide $40 by 20 to get a $2 per candle labor rate. When you apply the $2 labor cost to the $2.50 content cost, you get $4.50 per candle. This isn't a great example because you'll need to pay for other expenses like the additional utilities needed to produce the candles and the expense of importing supplies like boilers, pots, and jugs.

How much should you charge for candles?

This is based on the sort of brand you choose to be affiliated with. If you intend to sell bulk candles at a low price, you should expect your company to turn out a huge amount of low-cost candles with a slight but steady profit per candle. Votive candles are cheap and can be ordered for as little as $0.50 each. This approach can be very successful, particularly when several cheap candles are purchased in bulk, resulting in several sales for each customer. The drawback is that you would have to bring in a lot of money to make a big profit. You'll almost definitely need to expand, recruiting someone to help you achieve your broad production goals. Another choice is to create your brand. This means catering to a more discerning public able to pay a premium price for a candle. Some high-end artisanal candles will cost upwards of $200 each. For a brand, you'd have to worry about the packaging theme and what you're encouraging your clients to do with their candles.

3.3 Benefits of candle making business

If you've ever visited a big shopping center, you've probably seen a variety of candle shops. There are whole areas devoted to candles in several major department stores. To give you an example of how strong the candle business is, over 1 million pounds of wax are used to produce candles for the US market alone every year. The candle industry is worth around $2.3 billion a year without additional products such as candlesticks, ceramic pots, and so on. Who makes the most candle purchases? Seasonal holidays account for just 35% of overall sales, making them an outstanding all-year-round investment. Outside of these days, candles are purchased for 65 percent of the year. The most popular motives for buying a candle as a present include a seasonal gift, a housewarming gift, a dinner party gift, a thank you gift, and adult birthday presents. People nowadays believe fragrance to be the most important consideration when buying a candle. Make sure the candles you're thinking of selling have high-quality scents since this can be the difference between success and failure in the candle industry.

Conclusion

In 1969, in a period when India's domestic detergent industry had very few competitors, predominantly multi-national firms, which targeted the affluent of India, Karsanbhai launched Nirma. The detergents were not affordable for most middle-class and poor citizens. Karsanbhai began producing detergent powder in the backyard of his home in Khokra, near Ahmedabad and selling it door to door for Rs 3 per kg, while other brands were charging Rs 13 per kg. Business Standard reported how Karsanbhai came up with a genius idea during the early 1980s, when the Nirma was still struggling with the sales, for drying out market of the goods collecting all the due credits. This was accompanied by a huge ad campaign featuring his daughter singing the iconic Nirma jingle in a white frock. Customers were flocking to markets, only to return empty-handed. Karsanbhai flooded the industry with his goods as the demand for Nirma peaked, leading to huge sales. Nirma's sales peaked that year, making it the most successful detergent, well outselling its closest competitor, Hindustan Unilever's Surf. As Karsanbhai purchased the cement firm LafargeHolcim for 1.4 billion dollars that year, he showed once again that the business appetite is away from over. Mint reported how the deal in Rajasthan and the surrounding area would help Nirma achieve a stronger grip. While a media-shy guy, Karsanbhai, an entrepreneur in the truest sense, has a sharp eye for nation-building. In 1995, he founded the Nirma Institute of Technology, which was followed by the Nirma University of

Science and Technology, which was founded in 2003 and is supervised by the Nirma Education and Research Foundation. He initiated the education project Nirmalabs in 2004, aimed at educating and incubating entrepreneurs in India. Karsanbhai Patel received the Padma Shri award in 2010. Just like Nirma, you can also transform your soap and candle-making business into large corporate businesses with the help of your ingenious marketing and creative skills, dedication, perseverance, and unfearfulness of new and challenging situations.

Private Label Crash Course

Build Your First 6-Figure Business Supported by a Collection of 9+1 Profitable Strategies. Find the Best Products, Build an Enlighten Team and Start Your Personal Brand

By

Nespy Online Marketing

Table of Contents

Introduction	146
Chapter 1: Getting Started-Private Label	151
1.1 What is Private Label?	152
1.2 Private Label Categories	152
1.3 Different types of Private Label as profitable strategies	153
1.4 White Label vs. Private Label Dropshipping?	154
1.5 Dropshipping Private Label	157
1.6 Deciding What to Private Label	159
Chapter 2: Profitable Strategies in Building Six-Figure Business	166
2.1 Private Label for Profitability	166
2.2 9+1 Pricing Strategies	170
2.3 Best Practices in Private Label Branding	175
2.4 Positives and Negatives of Private Label	178
2.5 Keys to Private Label Greatness	180
Chapter 3: Finding the Products & Starting Your Personal Brand	**185**
3.1 How to Start Your Private Label Brand from Scratch?	186

3.2 Understand the costs of private labeling — 188

3.3 Choosing the Right Products — 198

3.4 Building a Team and Starting your Personal Brand — 201

Conclusion — 207

Introduction

A private label is where a person or corporation paying another business to make a commodity without its name, emblem, etc. The person or business then applies to the packaging their name and design. So, what sorts of items should be labeled privately? From skincare and dietary treatments and infant essentials, pet products, and kitchen utensils, pretty much all under the sun. The benefit of private labeling is that nothing innovative needs to be produced or developed by you. You can add your mark on it as long as it's not a proprietary commodity and label it yours. For the last ten years, private labels have risen by at least double the number of popular household products. In reality, there is a lot of conversation about the rise of private labels or retail brands around the world these days. Or we need to claim private brands, maybe since they are indeed labels by the end of each day. Opportunities to have ever-better-value offerings for both of us as consumers. Possibilities for everyone to push the main factors transforming the world of today and tomorrow. Yes, it's not the Private Label curse. It could well, in truth, be a present. A blessing that pushes us all to question the status quo again. A gift that pushes one to step positively with some of the main big forces that form the world of today to collaborate together more successfully and collaboratively. A blessing that is increasingly important to all of us, whether in the United Kingdom, the United States, China, or Scandinavia. If we like it or not, Private Label will soon have a single category of quick products in the country. In the last ten years, private labels have risen at least double the amount of popular consumer packaged goods brands. How did the Private Label expand at the above remarkable pace, and what lessons does it give players in the more narrowly established markets of fast-moving consumer goods? We like to think of it as a food event, but it's increasingly a complete experience of consumption. Flavors' globalization, marketers, and individuals have made Private Label a global fact. More and more, Private Label is the face of today's retailer. Comprehend it. This isn't going to go away. Act about it. Perhaps we should name them PRIVATE Companies from now on. Perhaps we might create very different tactics to survive if we began naming them brands instead of labels. Brands are concerned about combating their closest competing brand. Will they behave as though their closest advertised rival is the Private Label? Maybe they could, because maybe if they did, they might behave very differently in reality. The commodity has gone on. In turn, as Private Label has become a brand power in its own right, it has become privatized. It cannot be ignored as a single mark anymore. It's something a ton more. While taken out of context, Private Label is turning controversial for this cause, maybe more than any other, placing owners on the backhand side and retail section on the offensive. Neither group appears especially keen to publicly address it or cooperate on something outside development. Products have brought copycatting stores to court, and dealers have de-listed popular brands from their racks. There's a tiny concession space. It increasingly distorts agreed shopping habits and usage trends in order to exacerbate problems more. It is a brand that can often account for two out of three physical transactions made by your consumer. A brand that is gradually seen as an alternate product and value of parity. A company that will out-weigh and out-image any typical brand by exploiting the retailer's corporate strength and spending. A brand that can drive producers into a vicious cycle of loss in the market. A trillion-dollar market that, as you realize its sheer scale and future effects, must be the least evaluated and poorly understood industry around. An industry that in the years to come is going to get a lot larger. There would theoretically be billions of dollars of sales redirected by brand owners to this power. Are you confident your plans are ready? The remedies? But, as the solution, what do people recommend? Lower costs, increase efficiency, and be more imaginative. This is not just a remedy that you can pursue as a standard component of your business growth. It is simply not sufficient. This is an opportunity that requires the unusual and the unconventional. Or else rise to the challenge. The Private Label is a wake-up call from a brand creator. Wake up to the truth in the company. Wake up in search of a shopper. Wake up to what you might theoretically do for your company. Wake up to proactivity for real. Wake up to a chance to get the rest of the planet back into communication with your company. Private label has arisen from the conventionally held assumption that firms will benefit and conquer the competition by providing either higher value at a higher cost for their consumers (or shoppers) or fair value at a cheaper cost (retailer brands). In other terms, it's a preference between distinction (or innovation) and low cost, and it's safe to assume that only then have retailers fallen into the former to offer the latter to the shopper reliably in spades. As Coke (and Tesco) can also inform you, it pays dividends to see the brand on any street corner. However, as some of our research highlights would demonstrate, there is still a significant perception difference between Private Label and existing manufacturer labels in terms of quality/value. As long as the shopper is concerned, at least, without the other, one will not thrive, and broadly speaking, maker labels are better positioned to offer sound 'innovation' and 'value' to retailers. Just 16% of shoppers in all regions sincerely agree that a supermarket of retailer-owned goods can only be expected in the future. So, we think there is a potential for brands to constantly reinvent themselves through shopper intuition, deeper brand commitment, and creativity. The potential for retailers to continuously add value is there. The potential exists for producers to maximize their manufacturing ability and for interactions to be reinvented by agencies. But most critically, the potential is there to constantly impress and entertain the shopper, far beyond all their hopes. The other alternative frequently provided is to get yourself into making a private label. However, you may be compelled by Private Label to analyze the very simple essence of the company in which you are and to doubt whether it is strong enough to move you further. Ask for your goods. Ask how and to whom you are offering. Ask if you still are tuning into the agents of transition. Your corporate purpose issues. Ask if you have the best staff and processes to meet this crucial problem. Finally, Private Label is a concern for manufacturers alike. Knowing how to profitably manage it without undermining the very essence of the organization you are with. And the manufacturers that you work with. Yes, you may assume that you can survive without them. Yet we're advising, be very, very patient. If you want to be a genuinely successful marketing tool in terms of bringing to the shopper, you need one another. In comparison, we exist in an age in which the newspapers are building up major global supermarket chains as the latest businesses to despise. Why are you stopping this? As the messenger, you use Private Label, a messenger that not only reveals that you deliver excellent value and costs but also indicates that you think for your consumer and their long-term social needs. And you are really doing what you can to support them. Now, even more on this. The private label is, to a great degree, a hidden force. The conservative nature of the subject-matter literature tends to downplay its actual place in the world, a function far from conservative in fact, and a role in which Private Label is undeniably the single greatest influence on our businesses and goods today. Brands, engagement professionals, and scholars have consistently ignored or underestimated this. That's got to change.

Chapter 1: Getting Started-Private Label

A private label is where a person or corporation paying another business to make a commodity without its name, emblem, etc. The person or business then applies to the packaging their name and design. So, what sorts of items should be labeled privately? From skincare and dietary treatments and infant essentials, pet products, and kitchen utensils, pretty much all under the sun. The benefit of private labeling is that nothing innovative needs to be produced or developed by you. You can add your mark on it as long as it's not a proprietary commodity and label it yours. A private label product is made and marketed under a retailer's brand name through a contract or third-party maker. You specify all about the commodity as the distributor-what goes into it, how everything is packaged, what the logo looks like-you pay to get it manufactured and shipped to your shop. This is in relation to purchasing goods with their corporate logos on them from other businesses. A successful brand identity can be the crucial base for building loyal customers, customer growth, and a competitive edge. Care of your corporate name as your company's face is how you are viewed by the audience. Without a detailed, excellently defined brand identity, the consumer might not realize who you are. In the end, you need to create a personal link. The potential exists for producers to maximize their manufacturing ability and for interactions to be reinvented by agencies. But most critically, the potential is there to constantly impress and entertain the shopper, far beyond all their hopes. The other alternative frequently provided is to get yourself into making a private label. However, you may be compelled by Private Label to analyze the very simple essence of the company in which you are and to doubt whether it is strong enough to move you further.

1.1 What is Private Label?

A private label product is made and marketed under a retailer's brand name through a contract or third-party maker. You specify all about the commodity as the distributor-what goes into it, how everything is packaged, what the logo looks like-you pay to get it manufactured and shipped to your shop. This is in relation to purchasing goods with their corporate logos on them from other businesses.

1.2 Private Label Categories

Almost every consumer product category has both branded and private label offerings, including:

- Condiments and salad dressings
- Cosmetics
- Personal care
- Frozen foods
- Dairy items
- Beverages
- Household cleaners
- Paper products

1.3 Different types of Private Label as profitable strategies

Generic Private Label

Generic private-label goods are one of the conventional private label tactics used to provide the price-conscious consumer with a low-price alternative. The brand doesn't matter to these consumers. With limited advertising and no marketing, the goods are inexpensive, undifferentiated, poor inconsistency. In commoditized and low-involvement goods, these private labels are primarily present. For both discount stores in Western nations, this technique is widespread.

Copycat Brands

In order to draw buyers, manufacturers play on the price point, retaining the packaging identical to a national brand that offers a sense of the product's similar consistency. These goods are reverse engineered, utilizing factories of identical technologies from national brand products. In wide categories that have a clear market champion, certain private labels are mostly present. In the detergent group, Massive Corporation blindly embraces the copycat brand approach. Detergents against rival products with identical packaging have been launched, albeit at a cheaper price.

Premium store brands

Retailers now have started utilizing private labels, rather than just as a pricing strategy, as a store point of difference. Premium store brands are valued higher and are also high in performance than the national brands. Here, the customer proposal is to be the greatest brand that money will purchase. In the retailer's shop, these products get influential eye-catching locations. In the advertising, the manufacturer insists on the excellent consistency of the goods.

Value innovators

Retailers manufacture goods that have all the value-adding characteristics and eliminate the non-value-adding characteristics in order to reduce costs, one point ahead of the copycat approach, and thus provide the customer with the best value deal. The danger of being imitated also rests in these labels. As it produces furniture under a modern market paradigm that involves self-service, assembling, and transporting yourself, Ikea is renowned for its better goods.

1.4 White Label vs. Private Label Dropshipping?

You can select between white label and private label dropshipping if you want to launch an online store. Both words define goods that have been branded by a reseller, but the two definitions very distinctly. Particularly to beginners, they may seem quite complicated, so let's go through each one and explain their relative benefits.

Private Labeling

Private marking is where a company selectively makes a commodity for a store that offers it under its own name. Costco utilizes private marking, for instance, by marketing its own "Kirkland" brand that no other store can offer. As a consequence, goods with private labels are typically less pricey than national brands. Plus, they can be very lucrative if they're promoted properly. Dropshipping is a convenient method for private-label goods to be distributed. You will find a dropshipping provider if you are an online shop owner who can offer items directly to you and incorporate your branding. Dropshipping is an e-commerce market concept in which no inventory is held by the manufacturer. The retailer, instead, manages the packaging, packing, and delivery of goods to the end customer. In other terms, for dropshipping, the goods are delivered directly to consumers, and they are never used by stores.

White Labeling

A white-label product is a manufactured product that a company makes but is rebranded by marketers to make it look as though it had been produced. Each dealer is authorized to resell the item under its own title and labeling. Unlike private labels, several retailers may market a white-label commodity. For e.g., you can have your own branding and labels on the goods that are delivered if you wish to market a product under your brand name utilizing the dropshipping business strategy. It is often safer to search at something that already has a market when it comes to items with a white mark. It's dangerous to produce goods with white marks that consumers are not comfortable with. It's safer to go for existing brands that people regularly use. As with private labels, dropshipping makes it simple to market online white-label goods. Again, the items are delivered directly from the producers to customers, and the commodities are seldom seen by dealers.

Advantages & Disadvantages of White Labeling

You won't have to go through the complicated logistics of making a commodity in one of these two e-commerce market models. You can save a lot of time and money without significant expenditure of time and energy in product design and production. In essence, you will concentrate on selling the commodity to the target group and branding it. In order to expand your company, you won't spread yourself thin and can concentrate on other areas of expertise. So, let's go through the common advantages and disadvantages of each business model:

Advantages of White Labeling

There are some real benefits of the white labeling market model, including:

- **It saves time and money.**

It's just cheaper to white mark an established commodity instead of wasting resources on developing a product from scratch.

- **Gain a large profit**

In general, white label goods are exclusively marketed by suppliers and may be bought at cheap market rates.

Disadvantages of White Labeling

There are, on the other side, some risks of white marking, including:

- **Limited options for branding**

Because it will be the producer or retailer who makes the white label product's bottle, label, and packaging, depending on the concept, you can just decide what it will deliver for you.

- **Limited choices of products**

Just the goods that the maker produces will be preferred, and you will not be allowed to produce anything special to the market.

- **Competition is tough**

It is challenging to stand out from the other online vendors that, white-label or not, sell the same items.

1.5 Dropshipping Private Label

We have addressed that different dropshipping products are among the simplest methods for private or white label items to be distributed. So, let's go about how private or white label items can be dropshipped.

Finding a supplier

In order to achieve the sustainability of online shops, having a successful dropshipping supplier is utterly crucial. In quest of finding a directory of dropshipping vendors who sell private label facilities, you should look at business websites or just do a search on Google. Seeking a niche will allow you and your business to stand out from other retail vendors. Make sure that you conduct consumer analysis to figure out what sort of thing you would prefer to rebrand or distribute.

Establishing the identity with the brand

A successful brand identity can be the crucial base for building loyal customers, customer growth, and a competitive edge. Care of your corporate name as your company's face is how you are viewed by the audience. Without a detailed, excellently defined brand identity, the consumer might not realize who you are. In the end, you need to create a personal link. Brand awareness must be expressed in the products, slogan, website, and packaging. It can offer a' derived from human attributes' to your brand. Brands with a very well-established personality make the brand intimately relatable, connecting consumers at a relational level and having to have the commodity in their lives. This is relevant for dropshipping products, including the private and white labels.

Increase awareness about your label and brand

Growing your brand recognition is another important move towards building a profitable brand. If the product is fresh, then identifying your target customers and discovering ways to draw consumers to your shop is the very first thing you'll want to achieve. This is so if it's the private label dropshipping goods. Here are some forms that brand recognition can be improved without any expense:

- Build content on your website with the addition of a blog

- Developing your social network online identity

- To engage and network with more clients and get product feedback.

- To maximize your keyword scores, perform SEO.

1.6 Deciding What to Private Label

You might be wondering about what's a competitive commodity to private label. The secret to this phase and probably the most crucial step in beginning a private label company is researching and putting efforts into finding a good product. You ought to figure out which products/services are in the market to ensure if your product would sell. To see what people, look for on the internet and get ideas about what you can offer from there, you can use programs available online. If you intend to launch your private label company on online marketplaces, you'll want to use a testing method that actually monitors what individuals are searching for on that platform. For this, popular programs include Helium 10 and Jungle Scout. They both provide several resources to help you continue your market path with your private label.

What Makes A Good Private Label Product?

The biggest point to hold in mind when applying for a private label for a commodity is to find one that:

It is in strong market demand and has limited competition from sellers.

This can help you stop being trapped with things that you will not offer.

Has a strong margin for benefit

Taking into consideration how much the item would cost you vs. how much you will market it for. If the item is held in a warehouse, plus the expenses involved with sale online, don't neglect to take into account the delivery costs from your source to you and from you to your client, packing and storage fees.

If you can manage the expenses

If you have a $1,000 or $10,000 startup investment budget, you need to take into consideration how many units you will need/want to buy and how much of the budget you will spend.

How to Find Suppliers

It's time to search for a producer or trade firm that provides private label service once you have a commodity in mind that you would like to private label. You can select anywhere in the world to make your goods. And several times, the type of service/product you select would rely on where you choose to get your product made. For e.g., China might be worth considering if you are trying to sell toys or gadgets because they seem to produce a ton of these types of items at very low prices. Consider looking for Alibaba or AliExpress if you want to go on this path. Both of these platforms are bulk markets where the goods are identified by suppliers and trade houses, where you can find almost everything. Because with all our federal rules, it's a great choice to source in the U.S. whether you want to offer food, dietary foods, cosmetic goods, or something else you bring in or on your body. Check on Google for items sourced domestically. Say you're searching for vegan deodorant source, just type in Google "vegan perfume private label U.K." to get a list of companies that can use vegan deodorants for private label.

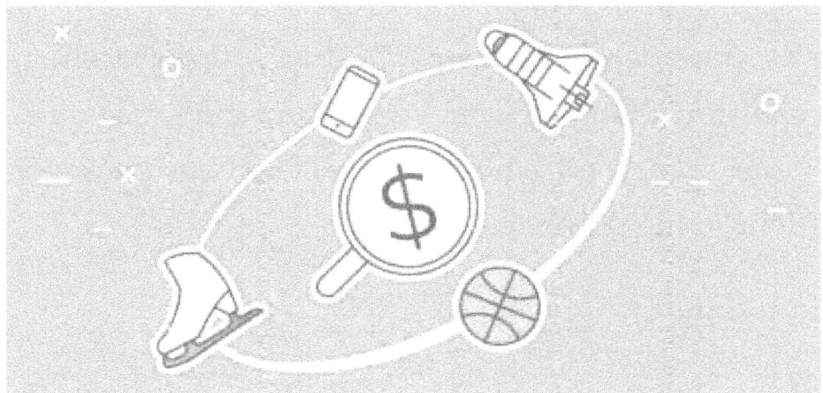

What to Ask Private Label Suppliers

Once you've drawn up a list of possible vendors, calling each one and posing some questions is a smart idea.

Pricing Per Unit

The price would usually already be accessible for you to see on the website for each item. However, depending on how many units you order, most manufacturers give a discount. Knowing this data would also assist you in estimating the gross margin.

MOQ

In the private label/wholesale environment, this is a generic word used because it stands for "minimum order" or the minimum number of units you will order at a time. On their website/product listing, most vendors will mention their MOQ, although you will only have to inquire for some. The MOQ of a producer can be as few as five units, although it can be 1,000 and beyond for some. Although this may be negotiable often, asking this upfront is a smart move so that you can prepare and budget appropriately.

Customization

It is nice to know what the factory is and will not do in advance so that you can stop trying to swap vendors later unless you are seeking to apply your branding to the package, customize packages, or make modifications to the product.

Production Time

It is helpful to know how long it would take your provider to meet orders when your private label company continues to expand, and you continue to prepare for potential orders. Typically, the norm is around 15 days (depending on the commodity and order size), so it can go up from there.

Response Time

Take notice of how long it takes for the supplier to get back to you, bearing in mind that you are initiating a long-term future trading partnership. You would want to make sure that your communication individual is trustworthy, prompt, and specifically addresses your questions. If your provider is based in another country, take into consideration that they are in a separate time zone and that you will not automatically obtain a reply. During their business hours, being present will allow the operation easier.

Samples

Ask for prototypes such that the consistency and particular requirements can be measured. Many vendors can submit a sample free of charge, while others may start charging a small fee. Anyway, it's certainly not something you'd skimp on, especially if you're trying to give the highest service to your customers.

Customizing Your Product

In how your product can market, customizing your product will play a huge role. Question yourself, "What's going to set my version apart from the competition?" The response to this is key in having a prospective customer select your product over the product of a more known, well-reviewed business. Perhaps it's as quick as providing color combinations or getting fancy packaging, or it might be easier to enhance a function that you want more in-depth. Such customizations, such as packaging upgrades, are likely to be achieved by your supplier, and some can be accomplished through yourself or by your suppliers, such as custom marking with product specifics and a logo. Customizing the goods in any form is the main message here. Stand out by having it different (and better) than the rivals '. By basically slapping the mark on it, you don't want to sell the same exact thing as another brand.

You are selling your Private Label product.

You may pick anywhere to market your private-label line of items. Here's an extensive list of online sales places or suggestions on how to get into shops.

A Personal Online Store

Such customizations, such as packaging upgrades, are likely to be achieved by your supplier, and some can be accomplished through yourself or by your suppliers, such as custom marking with product specifics and a logo. Customizing the goods in any form is the main message here. Stand out by having it different (and better) than the rivals '. By simply yanking your tag on it, you wouldn't want to give the same product as yet another brand.

Brick-And-Mortar

Sitting the goods on the shelf of a physical shop offers consumers the ability to see your product that they would never have dreamed of it otherwise. In other words, customers have to practically "search" for services or products they want to buy online. But if they don't think about it, they're not going to search and probably won't find it unless you pay serious bucks promoting it. If shoppers are still in a shop and happen to see it, it builds brand/product recognition at least. Fees and requirements for getting shelf-space vary by store, but it can be a decent place to start from local, family-owned stores. Read more regarding boutique collaborations or having your own storefront.

Markets

Markers and art fairs for producers are on the increase. Consumers love to shop locally and want to help their community's artisans. They're a perfect way to get instant input from customers, too. Find out how to start trading and find craft markets at farmer's markets.

Don't limit yourself.

Start with a variety of channels, in-person shops, and websites. You would be able to see over a span of time how many sales you create from each one, how much money each produces, etc. You should just stick doing what's profitable, then. It is certainly a road to launch your private label company, and it will be months until you can bring the goods on the market. But the trip can be well worth it if you do your product testing, pick the best source, separate the product from the market, and price it right.

Chapter 2: Profitable Strategies in Building Six-Figure Business

For private-label products, manufacturers may raise gross margins by managing the whole supply chain from manufacture to distribution. Clothing traders have been pushing different private-label options for years. Costco has the Kirkland private-label name. Nordstrom's got Caslon. And Kohl's has Sonoma as its in-house, billion-dollar brand. Although online stores have supplied other industries with private label labels, basic products for tangible products focused on low-cost hardware and office equipment, the move to clothes implies a brazen policy expansion. Any volume seller is looking at the advantages of growing private-label brand's goods in order to drive sustainability and connect with a more aware and conscious millennial generation who are known for not being very brand loyal.

2.1 Private Label for Profitability

Profits are powered by private labels. A private-labeled commodity or product with parity in operation and consistency with major labels will cost manufacturers 40 to 50 percent less to develop and sell to consumers. In order to negotiate with online marketplace empires and other online suppliers who offer low-cost products without caring about reducing margins, merchants will then switch around to provide greater discounts. Online, where customers have 100 percent pricing transparency, this is especially essential. This functions on both luxury and commodity items. Building and maintaining a private label often enables manufacturers to develop exclusive goods for higher prices or to manufacture commodity products below brands at a sustainable price. To boost their inventory rotation, manufacturers are now using private-label tactics. Retail stores with services from private labels could also have more than four seasons a year. An innovative team in private label, such as the JCPenney team of 250 designers working in-house or the internal production and procurement departments of Nordstrom, will contend on an equal footing with fast-trending fashion stores like H&M.

Factors to be Considered

It may be dangerous to hop into this business without carefully thinking it over. Before investing and dedicating time to a privately-label approach, here are some factors to be considered:

- **Identifying low cost and high-quality manufacturer**

A colossal advantage is strong production suppliers, while poor manufacturers or suppliers are a horrific liability. Spend the effort to do it correctly. There are hundreds or thousands of suppliers capable of producing stuff that you would need. Find the producer that fits all the requirements for price and consistency; often, identifying the markets that are relevant. You may also want to learn from Portugal or Vietnam for clothing. Vietnam, South Korea, and China have manufacturing expertise in electronics. Take note that costs for suppliers differ greatly depending on the order's size.

- **Strengthen the Skills in Design and Procurement**

The private label includes relationships with producers of agricultural and consumer goods, component retailers, multinational warehouses, and distribution suppliers. Will you broaden the current partnerships between suppliers? If not, determine whether to consult the staff or purchase the expertise that will render the retail company a key competency of the strategy regarding the private label. Consider a completely dedicated bet on vertical trading, too.

- **Using brand pricing and external signs as guiding principles for pricing policy**

Research your rival brands closely while designing your own products under the banner of a private label. Retailers ought to make up their mind whether to generate the product as a luxury product and expend marketing expenses or to position it as an alternate brand by selling below national labels. If product attributes can be readily contrasted and placed as a substitute brand, it is important to consider the price point of comparable goods to position them correctly against competitors' national brand/products label brands. In other situations, were comparing features is not something very straightforward. Retailers can use a number of internal market pointers for pricing, such as site traffic, ratings, consumer feedback, and retailers can recognize the popularity of the product. Today, if a commodity is popular/interest-generating, but the converging performance is low, this can cause a price reduction/promotion intervention.

- **Acknowledge the differences in categories and manage them smartly**

Consumers can browse for functionality within a particular perceived cost sub-set for white and hard goods. Buyers searching for features are opting for a dryer or washing machine. Potential customers are looking for other qualities, such as cloth, shape, trendiness, for soft items like clothing. Those features deter similarities.

- **Decide Efficient Customized Label Blend**

The best combination of private label and branded items has to be determined by retailers. Are buyers looking for a feature in a certain product category or range on the website? Collecting web search data can help marketers make a choice. They have to remember the client base as well. If the consumer pool is predominantly 28- to 51-year-old buyers, private label goods can be more value aware and prefer small-scale proliferation.

- **Implement Algorithmic, Data-Driving Pricing Methods**

With constantly evolving customer preferences, at every given level in time, you should be able to recognize demand levels and continually seek the optimum price value. Factor in leveraging algorithms based on technology systems to easily evaluate price levels and strategies; when priced carefully with supporting data, private-label brands also deliver unexpected revenues. For e.g., the commodity was priced well below the national brand by a generic manufacturer of merchandise with a very well private label refrigerator brand, just to experience a drop in revenue. The store began checking multiple price ranges, steadily pushing up the segment. Sales started to fall with the first $200 onwards. And, magically, revenue and traffic boomed until the price reached a hidden barrier. This sounds counterintuitive, but the private-label company has already been put in a competitive area with national labels in the view of the consumer. Instead of seeing it as a lower quality commodity, clients began to see it as domestic brands. They were prepared to move since the price levels were always cheaper than domestic brands. In a considerably more profitable buyer zone, it was repositioned by moving the idea up the continuum. If consumers interpret things the same way with analytic pricing, the same SKU will gain double the profits. These are some of the most important elements in successfully initiating your private label initiative at any major retailer. Going over these basics will strip the efforts of the bulk of danger.

2.2 9+1 Pricing Strategies

Want to maximize profit on your product sales?

Aside from other publicity and business tactics, a strong pricing policy is indeed something you need to concentrate on. When setting the price for your goods or services, what considerations do you consider? When determining the prices for your goods or services, there are a number of considerations, including:

- Production cost

- positioning strategies

- competitor's products

- Distribution cost

- Target consumer base

When buying a commodity, price is a very important consideration for a buyer. A productive pricing system can also have a profound influence on the company's performance. And often, it decides whether or not the organization can succeed. So, what are those tactics you should suggest in order to improve the revenue and be more profitable?

Premium Pricing

Marketers put rates higher than their competitors or rivals for this promotional policy. However, it is used where there is a major competitive edge, and a relatively cheaper price is safe for the marketer or the organization to charge. For small businesses that offer exclusive services or products, high pricing is perfect. A corporation, however, can check that the packaging of the goods, its promotional campaigns, and the décor or luxury facilities of the store all fit to maintain the fixed price.

- **Example of Premium Pricing**

Let's take the example of luxury specialty retail stores that charge you a little extra but sell you exclusive styles and tailored clothing.

Penetration Pricing

To try to draw buyers? Ok, this technique is going to help you with the purpose. Lower rates are given on utilities or goods under this strategy. Although this technique is used by many emerging firms, it does appear to lead to an initial reduction of profits for the business. Over time, though, the growth of product or service recognition will drive revenues and allow small businesses to stand out. In the long run, as a business succeeds in entering the sector, its costs always end up growing to represent the condition of its role in the sector.

Economy Pricing

The advertisement expense of a service or commodity is held at a low in this strategy. The technique is used during a certain period where the organization does not invest much in promoting the service or product.

Example of Economy Pricing

The first few budget airlines, for instance, are offered at low rates in discount airlines to fill in the jet. A broad variety of businesses, from discount stores and generic grocery manufacturers, use Economy Pricing. The technique, though, maybe dangerous for small firms when they lack the market scale of larger corporations. Small companies can fail to make a sufficient profit with low rates, but strategically tailoring price-cuts to your most loyal customers or consumers may be a successful way to guarantee their loyalty for years to come.

Price Skimming

This technique is meant to assist enterprises in focusing on the sale of innovative services or goods. During the preliminary process, this strategy means setting high prices. The rates are then reduced steadily when the competitor's goods or services arrive on the market. When the product is first released in the marketplace, this price approach produces an image of exclusivity and good quality.

Psychology Pricing

This method of pricing deals with a client's psychology. For e.g., setting the price of a ring at $99 is likely to draw more clients than setting prices at $100. But the concern is, in terms of a very limited gap, why are consumers more drawn to a product's former price? Psychology suggests that on a price tag, customers prefer to give greater attention to the first digits. When stores apply $0.99 on product tags of $1.99 or $2.99, you can find identical promotional strategies. The purpose of this approach, therefore, is to build an image of greater value for the consumer.

Bundle Pricing

How often have you been persuaded to purchase a multipack of 6 packets for $2.99 instead of purchasing one packet for $0.65? Or an SMS kit instead of texting on the individual rates? Without sacrificing efficiency, we all enjoy commodities that cost us less. This is why package selling is a success for both the vendor and the consumer and is profitable. The vendor gets to sell more of their inventory, and for less cost, the consumer gets to purchase the product in bulk. For instance, if bundle package of chips is for $1.30 and 3 multipacks for2.50$. The probability of purchasing three packs is more than purchasing only one. Bundle pricing enhances the worth sense when you are actually offering your consumers anything for free.

Value Pricing

This technique is used when external forces such as increased rivalry or unemployment cause corporations to offer valuable promotional offerings or goods, e.g., combo offers or value meals at KFC and other restaurants, to sustain sales. Quality pricing lets a buyer know like for the same price, they are receiving a ton of product. In several respects, profit pricing is analogous to economic pricing. So, let's make this very clear that there is added benefit with regard to service or product in value pricing. Generally speaking, price cuts should not rise in value.

Promotional Pricing

Promotional pricing is a really common method for sales and can be used in different department stores and restaurants, etc. Part of this promotional policy are methods such as money off coupons, Buy One Get One Free, and promotions.

Cost-based Pricing

This method entails determining cost-based rates for the commodity to be made, shipped, and sold. In addition, a fair rate of profit is usually added by the corporation or sector to compensate for the risks as well as initiatives. Businesses such as Walmart and Ryanair are seeking to become low-cost suppliers. These businesses may set lower rates by constantly lowering costs whenever feasible. This undoubtedly contributes to lower profits but better profits and revenues. Companies with higher costs can, therefore, often rely on this approach to pricing. Yet, in general, in order to demand greater profits and rates, these businesses purposely generate higher costs. The aforementioned techniques are the most widely adopted strategies used by corporations to increase profit from sales of their product or service. In its own unique way, any pricing strategy is effective. Therefore, consider your marketplace and other conditions before selecting a pricing plan for your good or service to bring the most out of the strategy used. Therefore, becoming mindful of the competitive place when setting a price is important. What the clients or buyers anticipate in terms of the price should be considered in the marketing mix.

2.3 Best Practices in Private Label Branding

Can you recall when generic or non-national branded items with large black lettering and bad product consistency indicated simple white or yellow packing materials? After the unmemorable early days of supermarket labels, stores have clearly come a long way. In fact, many private label labels today are practically indistinguishable from their producer-branded equivalents on the shelves.

Align with and support the master (retail) brand

It is certainly no accident that some of the best private label company portfolios are those that tend to be in tune with the supermarket master brand's positioning and strategic purpose. Preferably, their positioning is strongly complementary to the supermarket master brand, enhancing the latter's equity and beneficial relationships.

Bring differentiation to the category; fulfill unmet customer needs.

When their products are additive to the supermarket, or better still, the overall competition, private label labels are maybe at their strongest. One way to achieve this is to bring the category to something completely differentiated. Another similar approach is to resolve consumer expectations that are not fulfilled by the big national labels. Importantly, this difference can be more than just a cheaper price than the brands of the manufacturer. In the good or service offering itself, private label labels can often be exclusive. Safeway is a perfect illustration of introducing distinction to the market and thereby addressing an increasingly unmet desire of the customer. Finally, creativity is another form in which private label labels may offer category and consumer distinction.

Establish clear boundaries for private label brands

There is also a temptation to expand it everywhere and anywhere in the shop once retailers effectively establish a good private label brand. This extends horizontally across types of goods and vertically across ranges of price/value. However, the tendency to over-extend or dilute the private label brand properties is resisted by better practice retailers.

Define brands based on emotional attributes

Since they feel an intrinsic bond to them, customers prefer to gravitate towards (and stay faithful to) products. There is no more for products with private labels than for brands with national suppliers. For private label labels, it is important that they stand for something more than just price/value and much more than a commodity attribute. They need to have an emotional advantage to which customers may connect. This essential nuance is understood by marketers that have become popular with exclusive labels and find ways to distill emotional equity through their private label brands.

Distinguish brands with a distinct identity and appropriate brand linkages

Finally, a distinctive and highly identifiable visual identity is established by leading label labels and embraces a clear messaging approach. They still maintain clear rules specifying the degree to which the private label mark may and should be identifiably affiliated with the supermarket master brand. An attractive visual presence and strategically advantageous brand design are undeniably part of what makes private label companies popular or leads to their downfall if overlooked.

2.4 Positives and Negatives of Private Label

Advantages

There is a legitimate explanation for retailers that are involved in flooding their stores with items with their brand name. Many of the main benefits of goods with private labeling include:

- **Handling Production**

Third-party suppliers operate at the behest of the supplier, providing full influence over the ingredients and consistency of the goods.

- **Control overpricing**

Retailers may also assess sales cost and efficient selling due to leverage over the product.

- **Adaptability**

In reaction to growing consumer demand for a new feature, smaller stores have the opportunity to move rapidly to bring a private label product into development, whereas larger firms might not be involved in a product or niche category.

- **Managing branding Decisions**

The company name and package concept produced by the manufacturer carry private label items.

- **Managing profitability**

Retailers monitor the amount of profitability their goods offer due to control over manufacturing expenses and pricing.

- **Increased margins**

Private labels enable manufacturers to sell and raise the profit margin more competitively on their goods. Compared to producing brands, several manufacturers gain 25-30 percent higher profit profits on private labels.

- **Customer loyalty**

Nowadays, consumers want goods manufactured locally, and they would like more if they enjoy the private label products. You would be the only outlet who would be willing to supply them with such goods. It is challenging to win the trust of individuals in the retail sector.

Disadvantages

As much as you have the financial capital to spend in creating such a commodity, the risks of introducing a private label brand are few. Primary drawbacks include:

- **Manufacturer dependency**

Since the manufacturing of your product range is in possession of a third-party vendor, working with accomplished businesses is critical. Otherwise, if the manufacturer gets into challenges, you might lose out on opportunities.

- **Difficulty building loyalty**

In a number of retail stores, existing household brands have the upper hand and can always be found. Only in your shops can your goods be sold, restricting consumer access to it. Restricted supply, of note, may also be an asset, providing clients an incentive to come back and purchase from you. Although private label goods are usually offered at a lower price point than their brothers of the corporate name, certain private label brands are also branded as luxury products, with a higher price tag to show it.

2.5 Keys to Private Label Greatness

As of late, we are doing a lot of innovative work in the Private Label sector, and here is a good refresher of The Core Values that we believe in for developing our own labels that are strategically convincing. We also see that there are particular fundamental stories in their creation throughout all great store brand cases, but there are seven values that they must abide by to be genuinely strategically convincing.

Principles of Equity and Environment

From a branding and design point of view, there has never been more interest in the grocery store and how we connect, affect purchasing decisions, and even construct theatre inside it. This is real in every part of the world. Of course, there is a reverence we all have to have for the cultural uniqueness of the grocery store, from country to country, since some customers are in the store just once a week, to other food and market experience where customers connect every day. Even with these diverse regional variations in frequency, familiarity, and satisfaction inside the retail shop, there is a common emphasis on making the store brand function more credibly and more convincingly with consumers in general.

The equity connection

Immersing oneself in the retailer's overarching goal, its perception and equity distinction as it is now, and what is achievable in the future is important. To achieve this, the right branding collaborators coordinate with the senior brass of the distributors with which they operate, as well as the organization's top merchants and store name specialists. They take into account all the main targets for which a merchant is fishing and then see how to enhance store brands as being one of the key tools to accomplish their task. Store products strengthen the retailer's total equity and vice-versa, and they struggle because they do not.

Environmental support

A kit can only do too many. Your store brand will get overloaded if it does not have the off-shelf environmental help in the vast stream of 40,000+ items that many of the largest supermarkets carry today. Beyond the box, give it existence and speech. To help your brand, use the theatre in the shop.

Be preferential

For supermarket brands, own products, exclusive brands, and the like, there are loads of common nomenclatures. "But whatever the language, don't treat your store brands to the larger national brands as weaker "stepchildren. Don't be afraid to handle your supermarket labels preferentially in the store, beyond the incisive box template for your company. In their importance, in their distribution of space, in their positioning of shelves, and in their show and cross-merchandising all throughout the shop. No need to apologize to the CPGs or succumb to the study of planograms.

Don't blindly follow.

For years, there has been a "follow the herd" attitude of store labels, and today it still persists. Because of what Walmart has achieved with Such Prices, many retailers we talk to now are terrified of "white" packaging. So often, individuals are hyper-attentive to the competition and norms and what's going around the market of store labels. The bottom line is that you can build your own vision in a very creative and special way. Do not blindly obey the naming conventions, color conventions, or typically mundane price-centered store brands set by broad categories and how they have traditionally behaved in order to reconsider anything intelligently.

Three layers have to work together.

Make sure you are not concerned with visual language alone with the positioning of the store labels and how they are to be fully distinguished for the future. This is the responsibility of a number of production agencies, who feel they are only employed to rewrite the store brand's aesthetic vocabulary. If we want to encourage these products to be produced differently, we need to understand how the graphic language is created, indeed, but also how it is structurally packaged and the language we use to orally convey the item. Graphic, systemic, and verbal languages all cohesively operate together.

Steve Jobs never asked the consumer.

Apple is one of the world's most creative and well-thought-out, profitable enterprises. When questioned what Steve Jobs felt about research in a New York Times report and how Apple uses it to direct new product creation, he replied, "None... it's not the job of consumers to know what they want." There are so many retailers that use research to store products in their innovative development phase, and this is a mistake. Customers will still turn to the protection and what is comfortable with them, but if they are the only sounding board, you will not have the most creative performance.

On the brand's positioning

In using the name of the shop on the individual store brand packaging, there are no universal guidelines, just as there are no generalizations to create about how large the store brand should stretch. Both of these brands had a very definitive strategic positioning when producing Greenway, Hartford Reserve, and Via Roma for A&P, and this relationship that established the role of the company was a very significant part of the process. Clearly describe it, know that you want to distinguish the brand rather than sheer costs, own it thoroughly in the consumer's head, and correctly reiterate it. In the development of an ambitious store brand platform, these ideals would suit you well because they are standards that the best supermarket brands live by with true conviction. The name brand industry continues to be guided by continuing innovative creativity, a true steel hand in spreading out from the single "price" veil, and to be persuasive in their own right. And store brands need to be promoted with vigor, motivation, and media support.

Chapter 3: Finding the Products & Starting Your Personal Brand

You should concentrate on creating a reputation before you start your company, one that is recognizable and valued, and a private label benefits both you and the retailer or supplier you select. The first move with your organization is importing the goods you choose to market, products that do not crack easily, which have satisfaction for the customer. The second and most significant move is to make your brand known to current and future clients. The more customers remember your brand, the higher it is possible that your revenue rate will be. Through selecting producers or suppliers who will submit your goods via Private Label, you will help this along. This operates by encouraging the consumer to position their orders with you, then deliver them to the retailer and directly dispatching the product. The return home address would be that of the company in most situations, but for Private Label, this will be yours. This ensures that whether they have any concerns or queries, the consumer would assume that the service/product has come from you, and they will only contact you. This helps you build up a brand reputation, but using trustworthy vendors, depends on you, and you deliver top-quality customer support. In general, manufacturers are willing to use private labels since it suggests that they do not have to be interested in any consumer problems. To sum up, while you are looking to get your brand out and develop a company without leeching on mainstream online market place/websites' popularity, a private label makes perfect sense. It will require a bit extra time to select a supplier since you must do the job yourself and guarantee that you work for the right supplier. Still, you will also gain a better profit when you take responsibility for the client support and are willing to negotiate the supplier's rates. A private label is where a person or corporation paying another business to make a commodity without its name, emblem, etc. The person or business then applies to the packaging their name and design. So, what sorts of items should be labeled privately? From skincare and dietary treatments and infant essentials, pet products, and kitchen utensils, pretty much all under the sun. The benefit of private labeling is that nothing innovative needs to be produced or developed by you. You can add your mark on it as long as it's not a proprietary commodity and label it yours.

3.1 How to Start Your Private Label Brand from Scratch?

Because of its profitability and consumer benefits, private labeling has boomed in prominence in recent years. To distinguish between larger vendors, more and more sellers create their products on and off e-commerce marketplaces. With 50 percent of one of the online markets, private labeling vendors, the rivalry is fierce. You need to realize what you're doing if you want to excel. To start a strong private label, you need the know-how, expertise, and money. When you place your logo and name on a standardized commodity, private labeling is. This separates the brand from related rivals and retailers. You have full power over your brand, with a private label. You establish a distinctive identity that is essential for successful promotion and the acquisition of consumers. Customers, not goods, are faithful to labels. Customer satisfaction and repeat business may be created through the private label. In the market, you still have the power of your price and place. A private label on the online marketplace enables you to build a different collection of items only for your product. This gives real estate devoted to your brand and assures that you are not vying against other retailers for the Buy Box. Since they get higher value, clients love private labels. Private-label goods are usually cheaper, but major stores' efficiency is the same, if not higher. In reality, at least one form of private label product is purchased by approximately 98 percent of customers. Depending on their lifestyle, customers may even buy goods. One study showed that clients prefer private labels for the price and choose them based on expertise. They buy from private labels that they most associate with. Ultimately, in a sea of rivals, a private label separates the name, allows you greater leverage over your revenues, and appeals to a niche client target. So, you have agreed to launch a private label of your own. The measures to take to help you start a profitable private label from design to launch are below.

3.2 Understand the costs of private labeling

Before digging deeper into a private label, it's important to consider the initial start-up costs. In comparison to reselling, private tagging is more costly. However, this capital input usually results in a better return on your expenditure in the long term.

Manufacturing

Typical development expenses, such as supplies, processing, manpower, and transportation, would have to be accounted for. You may need to consider the customization charge, too. For customizing a product with your mark, packaging, or specs, most manufacturers will charge a fee.

Brand

Even to design the brand itself, you would require money. To create the logo and package template, you'll definitely want to employ a graphic artist. To stress the voice of your company, you will also want to develop a content strategy.

Marketing

Marketing is a significant part of private labeling. Customers don't know about your company, so to become more noticeable, you need to spread knowledge. A large cost may be generated through ads such as promoted and boosted blogs. A website creator and domain name would presumably both need to be charged for. For any other unforeseen fees or modifications that pop about at the beginning of the start of a new company, you can also add a sizable buffer.

- **Choose the products you want to sell**

The majority of corporations and labels start with a commodity. The brand is how you create your cash and profits. The item is the guiding force of your business. Starting a commodity with your name helps determine your margins, demand, and availability. The brand is the consumer service, but you will need to offer your consumers a valuable product in the end. You would typically choose a branded commodity that you place your own logo on while you market a private label. This suggests that a single generic product begins with your "brand." How do you further build and broaden your branding using that product? You want high-rank and high-margin units when buying a commodity. To lower warehousing and shipping costs, you will want thin, lightweight goods. If the first product you offer doesn't work out or you choose to shift paths, you can still move goods. The aim is to stick less to one commodity than to use product testing as a prism in your overall business and niche instead. You should also accept complimentary commodities with this in mind. If you market key items, you want to think of a range of similar goods that would still blend with your brand when choosing key products. For starters, you can grow inside the travel domain or beverage industry if you sell travel mugs. You will market some eco-friendly home products as well if you sell environmentally efficient cleaning products.

- **Define your target market**

Who is the perfect consumer for you? Who would be more willing to buy your unique product? This can assist you in deciding the sorts of goods you are trying to produce and how you are going to promote such products. The consumer is your market and your brand's secret. Getting a well-defined target demographic is more relevant than ever, considering the current condition of the economy. No one is willing to afford to target everyone. By approaching a niche segment, small enterprises may successfully compete with big firms. Many firms say they are targeting "anyone interested in my services." Others say they are targeting buyers, renters, or stay-at-home moms in small businesses. These priorities are all too common. Targeting a certain market does not mean that you exclude entities that may not follow the standards. Instead, focus marketing helps you to concentrate your advertising money and brand message on a single demographic that is more inclined than other markets to purchase from you. This is a means of meeting prospective consumers and creating a business that is far more accessible, accessible, and effective. For instance, an interior design business might opt to sell to households between the ages of 34 and 63 with incomes of $160,000-plus. The business could opt to approach only those involved in kitchen design remodeling and conventional designs in order to define the segment any better. This business may be broken into two niche markets: parents on the move and baby boomers leaving. It is much simpler to decide where and how to advertise your brand with a well-specified target audience. To help you identify your target market, here are some ideas.

Look at your current customer base.

Who are your new clients, and why are they buying from you? Look for features and desires that are popular. What ones do other businesses carry in? It is also possible that your product/service will also help other individuals like them.

Check out your competition.

What are your adversaries targeting? Who are the clients at present? Don't try the same business. You might discover a niche market they are missing.

Analyze your product/service

Write up a description of each of the product or service specifications. List the advantages it offers next to each function. A graphic artist, for instance, provides high-quality design services. The advantage is the picture of a professional organization. More clients would be drawn to a professional image when they perceive the business as professional and trustworthy. So, basically, attracting more clients and earning more profits is the advantage of high-quality design. When you have your advantages identified, make a list of persons that have a need that suits your benefit. A graphic designer may, for instance, opt to approach organizations involved in increasing their consumer base. Although this is already too common, you now have a foundation on which to proceed.

Choose specific demographics to target.

Find out not only who wants the products or service and also who is most willing to order it. Consider the reasons that follow:

- Location
- Education level

- Occupation

- Gender

- Ethnic background

- Marital or family status

- Age

- Income level

- Ethnic background

Consider the psychographics of your target.

Psychographics is a person's more intimate traits, including:

- Personality

- Values

- Interests/hobbies

- Attitudes

- Lifestyles

- Behavior

Assess how your service or product would blend with the lifestyle of your destination. How and where is the item going to be used by your goal? What characteristics are most enticing to your goal? What media for details does your goal switch to? Can the newspaper read the destination, check online, or attend unique events?

Evaluate your decision

Make sure to consider these issues after you have settled on a target market:

- Are there enough individuals that meet my criteria?

- Is my goal actually going to benefit from my product/service?

- Are they going to have the use for it?

- Do I know what guides my aim to make choices?

- Can they afford my service/product?

- With my post, may I meet them? Are they readily accessible?

Don't smash the goal so far down there. Know, there is more than one niche opportunity you may have. Consider how, for each niche, the marketing message can be different. If you can successfully hit all niches with the same post, then maybe you have broken down the market so much. Also, if you notice that there are only 50 individuals that match all of your requirements, you may need to reevaluate your objective. Finding the right combination is the trick. You might be wondering, "How do I gather all this data?" Attempt to look online for analysis that others have done on your aim. Look for posts and blogs in publications that speak to or around the target group. Check for blogs and sites where thoughts are shared by people in the target market. Check for sample findings, or try doing your own survey. Ask for input from the new clients. The hard part is identifying your target demographic. It is much simpler to find out which platforms you should use to attract them, and what advertisement campaigns can connect with them if you know who you are approaching. You should give it only to people that suit your requirements instead of delivering direct mail to anyone in your ZIP code. In identifying the target demographic, save money and have a greater return on investment.

- **Consider your differentiating factor.**

You've settled on demand and a commodity. Now, what is going to make you distinctive in your business from your competitors? Look at the rivalry. What is their emphasis? And where are they missing? A perfect spot for you to put the brand is the field that they struggle the most. You could find, for example, that all of your rivals have a formal language; with your brand, you might take a goofy and enjoyable tone. In order for it to become a good differentiator, it doesn't have to be a big improvement. The core of your identity becomes your differentiator. Keep in mind that price may also be a defining factor. You would get a different demographic and competition than a cheap or discounted commodity, whether you are quality or luxury product.

- **Create your brand look**

Your "brand" consists of the goods, the demand, and the distinguishers. Yet, it is your material and aesthetic as well. You need a clear emblem that represents the name while private labeling is used. How you are and where the stuff comes from, the logo tells. This emblem can be included in all communications, packaging, and marking. Be sure it's accessible as a corporation and website prior to picking the brand name. This would mean that you do not infringe on any patents or fight with companies with identical names. To build the logo and package template, you'll definitely want to employ a graphic artist. This is the perfect approach to make things look respectable and trustworthy to the private label.

- **Create an experience**

A brand is, ultimately, more than a slogan, though. Your "brand" is how your business is experienced by the client. It's a consistent way for your audience to communicate. You need to work out how consumers can uniquely perceive your brand based on brand differentiation. What is your content going to look like? What could you provide that is unique to the experience of your brand? You may produce visually enticing social media photographs, for instance, that contribute to the lifestyle around your dog collars. Or you should make sure that you react to and respond to any social network statement or post. To keep your label on the edge, you can use special and exclusive packaging. Build an atmosphere, and you can turn your one-time consumers into long-term customers.

- **Find a supplier**

Acting with a good provider is an important aspect of private marking. The manufacturer must have private labeling expertise so they can help you make a return from your products. For a variety of consumers, several overseas factories will produce a standardized commodity and modify such items with private packaging for marking. You collaborate with a retailer, for instance, that produces bottles of water and T-shirts. They have ten buyers, each with their own special emblem written on the bottles, that offer water bottles. A customization and packing fee will normally be paid by the factory.

- **Build the brand**

You have put yourself in a role, built a differentiator, and found a supplier. It's time to start developing your organization now. You have to:

- Name and image copyright.

- Website configuration

- Creating a voice on social media

- Shape an LLC

Just like you would like any other legal corporation, recognize your e-commerce firm. You need yourself, your goods, and your income to be covered. You would also like to start naming the lists with online items. A private label means you don't have to fight for a Buy Package. "With a different page for your branded goods, you hold your own "real estate." In line with the brand background, this is a good chance to customize the listing.

3.3 Choosing the Right Products

Choosing the best market and the right goods to spend your efforts on is the greatest challenge you would have to conquer. This decision is vital to the success or failure of your company. The only biggest mistake you're going to make is selecting a product based on your own interests or personal preferences, particularly if you want to create a genuinely profitable company. You have to provide what other customers want, not what you want. Especially if you are not the type of individual to embrace patterns or the type of individual that is always perceived to be "outside of the box." We can't tell you what products to offer, but we can definitely give you some ideas about how to pick the right ones.

How to choose the right product

Your organization would have an uphill struggle to become profitable without a strong product portfolio. It may seem impossible to try to find out what you are trying to market, with potentially millions of items out there. The item you chose will also pose other concerns that you may need to work on. For starters, shipping may become an issue if you are planning to sell freezers. Depending on where the clients work, whether you are selling alcohol, there could be regulatory limits. Market analysis can sound daunting, but knowing the product can cater to the people you are going to attract through your site is important. You should monitor the industry dynamics if you already have an understanding of what you intend to do to see how the commodity is actually performing on the market. If you are really not sure what you'd like to offer, trends can still be helpful to you. Business dynamics will offer you an indication about what items consumers are purchasing or are interested in buying at the moment. Look for items that address a dilemma the target group is experiencing. If your consumer is fed up with the current product range, open a unique and better product to deliver them. Choosing a commodity that is not reasonably available nearby or a national brand that is coveted by a region outside of where it is actually accessible may also be a brilliant choice. Another recommendation is to find a service/ product based on your target audience's interests. This may be in the shape of a new TV show that is beginning or a fashion trend. It often applies to aiming for a difference in chances. If you choose a product that many different competitors are already selling, find something that you can do differently or better than everybody else. This can be an enhanced product characteristic, a market that your competitors totally miss, and maybe something in your marketing plan. If you are trying to market a commodity-based on something that is trending at the moment, ensure that you capitalize early on the pattern. There tend to be more individuals who buy the product at the beginning of a trend. Everybody else is now also moving along to the next thing if you get on the hype train at the end of the trend. Do not wait too long to profit on a trend in the market unless you think that you're going to revive a dead trend. When you make your choices, it is important to take into account product turnover. It would take a lot of time and resources on a product range that varies year after year to guarantee that the product selection is held up-to-date and does not include last year's choices, which could no longer be eligible. A reduced churn product would enable you to engage in a more informative website that will be applicable for a longer time span.

Don't be frightened of looking at smaller segments and niches of products. Although there may be fewer prospective customers, there will also be less competition, making it easier to get it to the top of the search engines and much more cost-effective in terms of marketing. The right product is an essential part of your success. Take your time and also don't rush into the first good-looking product.

Looking for Product Ideas

There is no need to start a shop without a commodity to sell. Begin with something you already have, or how you can fix your own issues or the challenges of people you meet before you start looking for fresh ideas on what you can sell. There are some ways to consider:

- Which items or niches are you involved in?

- What items are your mates excited about?

- Which challenges do you have with your own life?

- Whose goods can address this?

- What kind of firms are based in your community?

- Can they be translated into a definition online?

- What will organizations in your culture cater to individuals outside of your community?

- In other areas of the planet, what items are trending?

- Is there a need inside your society for them?

- Will you build in your society a market for them?

- Is there a certain sector you like to be interested in if you are confused regarding products? In that industry, what products are popular?

- What items can you find useful from that industry?

- In other online retailers, what items are popular?

- Will this commodity have a niche that you should specialize in in sales?

- What's the social curation website trend?

- Is there an undiscovered thing out there that individuals would want to see open to them?

3.4 Building a Team and Starting your Personal Brand

Choosing the Right Supplier

It can be tricky to pick a supplier for your private label company, but it can help you to realize that there are a variety of suppliers who have been doing this for several years. Some lead the industry in broad industries, and this may be the perfect place to get started in your new company since the goods you offer are already established and have gained appreciation from the market. You can have to trade-off or work in restricted strategies with your profitability, and you need to be careful in reviewing the terms and conditions of each corporation, but each of these can create a backdoor into which you can start a profitable long-term business. Not all private labels are made equally, and to guarantee that your organization is effective, you want to make sure you chose the best provider. There are certain items that your provider wants to provide and some things that are less essential but can have greater convenience. Any of the items you'll be searching for in a provider include:

- Will the retailer have members who are knowledgeable?

- Will the supplier devote them to a particular entity committed to your account?

- Are they invested in being advanced technologically?

- How can you send orders?

- Where are they situated?

- Are they a coordinated business?

- How fast are their orders shipped?

- How are they keeping you throughout the loop on product returns and items out of stock?

- How fast can they send you the tracking details and purchase order?

- What payment types do they approve?

- What kind of fees are they charging?

It may seem impossible to locate the legal firms and distinguish them from the fraudulent as you are searching for a provider. There are some tricks to choosing a decent provider for private labels. One crucial point to bear in mind when you start approaching suppliers is that they could very well be the secret to selecting the best supplier, even though they are not the right match for you. Make sure you always ask every supplier you meet if they can guide you in the appropriate path to reach a supplier that suits your company. As they're in the business, they are sure to have connections that will help you and are typically prepared to share the details. Looking at social media is another way one can improve the chances of having a reliable supplier to deal with. Often, through a family member, neighbor, or acquaintance who might be in the industry or meet someone in the industry, you may find a lead. Any lead is a successful lead, even though it leads to a dead end. In order to strengthen the partnership, you have with your supplier, there are a few items you should do:

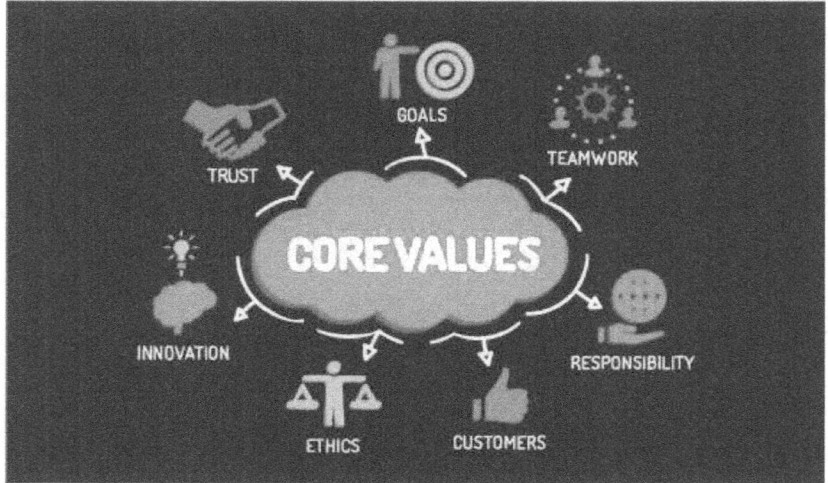

- Pay on time to develop trust and then become a reliable client.

- Set simple and realistic targets if an estimation of the goods you plan to sell in a specified period is requested

- Remember that they have other clients and do not belong to you alone.

- Learn what you need when you put orders to speed up the operation.

- If there is a malfunction, do not accuse the representative, but collaborate with them to find a remedy.

- Knowing somebody on a personal level seems to make them more likely to help you out. Build relationships with your delegate

- Train them to identify what you need, such as fresh product photos and product update updates, items out of stock, and products were withdrawn.

Finding the Right Suppliers and Working with Them

The one crucial part you have to do before you continue the quest for the right suppliers is learned how to say the difference between a true wholesale supplier and a department store that works like one. The manufacturer orders their stock from a genuine wholesaler and delivers far higher deals than a supermarket would. To create a good organization, you need to be able to do all of the following:

Have Access to Exclusive Distribution or Pricing

Being able to negotiate unique product agreements or exclusive prices would offer you the advantage without the need to import or produce your own product to sell online. These are not quick items to arrange, and you can notice that you are still out-priced, and at wholesale rates, some private label brands would still offer the same or equivalent. You need to find a way to persuade the buyers that the commodity you sell is of greater quality than the competitor, whether you can have exclusive distribution, particularly if the competition sells a knock-off product at a cheaper price. This is where the website's "about us" page becomes much more useful as it is a good way to share the fact that you are unique to the product.

Sell at the Lowest Possible Price

You will rob clients from such a chunk of your niche market if you are willing to sell your goods at the lowest costs. The main thing is that since you actually won't be able to appreciate the gain, you are destined to struggle. The low price is not often the primary motivating factor behind the choice of a consumer to shop. Customers seem to choose to invest their cash on the best benefit and lowest cost of a commodity. This suggests that you ought to persuade them that the best decision is to invest a little extra cash in your goods, so there is less downside and more appeal to them.

Add Your Value Outside of the Price

Think in terms of having data that complement the items selected. A real capitalist can fix challenges, and at the same time offering goods at high rates. In your unique niche, make sure you give suggestions and insightful recommendations. Your customer support is one extremely efficient way to bring value to the goods outside of the costs. If you are willing to address all the queries of your consumer without needing to call you and are willing to respond to any emails easily, your store website will stick out from the rest.

Conclusion

A private label is where a person or corporation paying another business to make a commodity without its name, emblem, etc. The person or business then applies to the packaging their name and design. So, what sorts of items should be labeled privately? From skincare and dietary treatments and infant essentials, pet products, and kitchen utensils, pretty much all under the sun. The benefit of private labeling is that nothing innovative needs to be produced or developed by you. You can add your mark on it as long as it's not a proprietary commodity and label it yours. Dropshipping is a convenient method for private-label goods to be distributed. You will find a dropshipping provider if you are an online shop owner who can offer items directly to you and incorporate your branding. Dropshipping is an e-commerce market concept in which no inventory is held by the manufacturer. The retailer, instead, manages the packaging, packing, and delivery of goods to the end customer. In other terms, for dropshipping, the goods are delivered directly to consumers, and they are never used by stores. There is a legitimate explanation for retailers that are involved in flooding their stores with items with their brand name. Third-party suppliers operate at the behest of the supplier, providing full influence over the ingredients and consistency of the goods. In reaction to growing consumer demand for a new feature, smaller stores have the opportunity to move rapidly to bring a private label product into development, whereas larger firms might not be involved in a product or niche category. You should concentrate on creating a reputation before you start your company, one that is recognizable and valued, and a private label benefits both you and the retailer or supplier you select.

The first move with your organization is importing the goods you choose to market, products that do not crack easily, which have satisfaction for the customer. The second and most significant move is to make your brand known to current and future clients. The more customers remember your brand, the higher it is possible that your revenue rate will be. Through selecting producers or suppliers who will submit your goods via Private Label, you will help this along. This operates by encouraging the consumer to position their orders with you, then deliver them to the retailer and directly dispatching the product. To sum up, while you are looking to get your brand out and develop a company without leeching on mainstream online marketplace/websites' popularity, a private label makes perfect sense. It will require a bit extra time to select a supplier since you must do the job yourself and guarantee that you work for the right supplier. Still, you will also gain a better profit when you take responsibility for the customer support and are willing to negotiate.

Lightning Source UK Ltd.
Milton Keynes UK
UKHW052004150321
380411UK00006B/1001